REFORMING SOCIAL POLICY

REFORMING SOCIAL POLICY

CHANGING PERSPECTIVES ON SUSTAINABLE HUMAN DEVELOPMENT

Editors

Daniel A. Morales-Gómez
Necla Tschirgi
Jennifer L. Moher

INTERNATIONAL DEVELOPMENT RESEARCH CENTRE
Ottawa • Cairo • Dakar • Johannesburg • Montevideo • Nairobi • New Delhi • Singapore

Published by the
International Development Research Centre
PO Box 8500, Ottawa, ON, Canada K1G 3H9

© International Development Research Centre 2000

Canadian Cataloguing in Publication Data

Main entry under title :
Reforming social policy : changing perspectives on sustainable human development

ISBN 0-88936-878-3

Includes bibliographical references.

1. Social policy.
2. Canada — Social policy.
3. Ghana — Social policy.
4. Chile — Social policy.
5. Sustainable development.
I. Morales-Gómez, Daniel A. (Daniel Antonio), 1946-
II. Tschirgi, Necla Yongacoglu, 1946-
III. Moher, Jennifer L. (Jennifer Lori), 1969-
IV. International Development Research Centre (Canada)

HD75.6R43 1999   361.2'5   C99-980280-1

All rights reserved. No part of this publication may be reproduced, stored in a retrieval system, or transmitted, in any form or by any means, electronic, mechanical, photocopying, or otherwise, without the prior permission of the International Development Research Centre. Mention of a proprietary name does not constitute endorsement of the product and is given only for information. A microfiche edition is available.

IDRC Books endeavours to produce environmentally friendly publications. All paper used is recycled as well as recyclable. All inks and coatings are vegetable-based products.

Contents

Preface – Daniel A. Morales-Gómez vii

Chapter 1
Introduction: The Paradox of Development
– Necla Tschirgi 1

Chapter 2
Ghana: Social-policy Reform in Africa
– Ernest Aryeetey and Markus Goldstein 9

Chapter 3
Chile: Progress, Problems, and Prospects
– Dagmar Raczynski 45

Chapter 4
Canada: Experience and Lessons for the Future
– Terrance Hunsley 83

Chapter 5
Conclusion: A Research Agenda for Social-policy Reform
– Jennifer L. Moher 115

Appendix 1
Acronyms and Abbreviations 147

Appendix 2
Contributing Authors 149

Bibliography 151

Preface

Persistent poverty, slow economic growth, labour-market difficulties, shifting demographics, and social insecurity are phenomena without borders. Despite unprecedented material progress in some countries, basic education, health care, housing, social safety nets, and social protection remain insufficient for the majority of the world's population.

Governments in developed and developing countries are thus reevaluating their social policies and programs, reexamining their social safety nets, and seeking new options in the reform of social-protection and social-welfare systems. To deal with the pressures on them, governments are experimenting with various approaches to changing public policies in the social sphere — experiments guided by altered principles and procedures for social-service financing, implementation, and delivery, as well as shifting divisions of responsibility among the state, the private sector, and nongovernmental actors. Not enough is known, however, about the outcomes of these experiments.

This book contributes to filling this knowledge gap and is the result of an activity undertaken by the Assessment of Social Policy Reform (ASPR) program of the International Development Research Centre of Canada. The ASPR program is global in its perspective, activities, and outreach. Its mission is to support applied research to provide developing-country governments and civil-society actors with the information, knowledge, and tools needed to evaluate the impact of options in social-policy reform and implement effective social policies and programs across sectors. The objective of this volume is to draw on the selected reform experiences of three countries — Ghana, Chile, and Canada — to identify key issues warranting future development-policy research. This book is expected to contribute to a better understanding of the processes of social-policy reform in diverse national economic, social, and cultural environments.

Daniel A. Morales-Gómez
Senior Scientist
International Development Research Centre

Chapter 1

Introduction

The Paradox of Development

Necla Tschirgi

The 20th century has been a remarkable age of material advancement and sociopolitical transformation. By any yardstick, people around the world have witnessed profound changes in their conditions of life. For example, the 1997 edition of the *Human Development Report* of the United Nations Development Programme (UNDP) painted an impressive picture of major advances in the last 50 years: infant mortality rates have dropped to less than 60 per 1 000 births (a reduction of nearly 60%); adult illiteracy has been cut in half; primary-school enrollment has come to include more than three-quarters of the school age population, with notable increases for girls; life expectancy has increased to the age of 40 for 75% of the world's population.

Yet, these impressive achievements stand in stark contrast to persistent poverty, striking inequities in the distribution of the benefits of development, and wide-scale social exclusion or marginalization. The report indicated that 1.3 billion people (mainly women and children) in the developing world live on less than 1 United States dollar (USD) a day; 800 million people are malnourished; disparities between the rich and the poor remain vast in most regions, particularly in Africa and Latin America. Nonetheless, the report maintained that the eradication of extreme poverty in the first decades of the 21st century is a feasible and affordable goal. However, it also makes it clear that to accomplish that goal, economic growth in the world's poorest countries needs to be accelerated, and governments, as well as other actors, need to implement policies to reduce poverty in their societies and promote human and social development around the world.

The annual issues of the *Human Development Report* and other similar studies provide a global report card by rating various indicators of development across geographic boundaries and socioeconomic systems. In doing so, they serve to underscore the inadmissibility of grave social deprivation in the midst of unparalleled material welfare in today's global society. More importantly, in dissecting the many dimensions of development and pointing to the linkages between them, such studies allow the emergence of a more integrated understanding of human progress and development. In the words of UNDP's James Gustav Speth, since the annual issues of the *Human Development Report* began to be published in 1990 they have been instrumental in "ending the mismeasure of human progress by economic growth alone" (UNDP 1996, p. iii).

There can be no doubt that, historically, economic growth has been instrumental in enhancing human welfare. However, history also confirms that the relationship between economic growth and human and social development is neither unilinear nor automatic. The emergence of "jobless growth" in a number of industrialized countries has, for example, given rise to widespread unemployment and to new forms of poverty and exclusion. Drastic financial crises in various newly industrialized countries have unleashed wide-scale social and political unrest. The negative environmental and health impacts of unrestrained material progress are amply established. The disruptive social, cultural, and political consequences of rapid economic growth have led to several problems, such as massive dislocations of populations, political upheavals, new health risks, crime, violence, and civil wars in various parts of the world. Technological and economic progress have also been instrumental in accelerating the cross-border transport of many development problems, such as drugs, crime, pandemics, and violence, thereby creating new security threats that supersede national borders.

The experience of the last 50 years shows that for development to occur, a complex set of factors needs to fall into place, and economic growth is only one of these factors. Higher levels of economic growth do not necessarily translate into increased social well-being or the eradication of extreme poverty for hundreds of millions of people excluded from development. In short, economic growth is no longer equated with development. Instead, in the closing years of the 20th century, it is accepted that development has multiple dimensions, encompassing human security, macroeconomic growth, environmental sustainability, and participatory governance.

For students and practitioners, the key challenge is not only to understand the complex and multidirectional links among the various dimensions of development but also to identify the extent to which, and ways in which, these can be reinforced through appropriate public strategies and policies. Indeed, one of the key concerns of development theory and research has been to understand how public policies and programs can be designed to address both persistent and newly emerging development problems. Until recently, however, countries regularly defined their development policies in terms of macroeconomic considerations. Even when governments assumed responsibility for traditional social sectors, their policies were considered derivative of, or residual to, broader economic policies. It has only been with the broadening of the concept of development that it has come to be acknowledged that public policies in such diverse areas as education, health, housing, human rights, and the environment have in their own right a direct bearing on the nature, direction, and outcomes of a country's development efforts. Both governments and development agencies have increasingly come to recognize the need to put people at the centre of development and to give development a human face. They have begun to advocate strategies to explicitly address social-development needs.

Yet, there has been relatively little research that systematically examines the roles and impacts of noneconomic policies in development. Without historically rooted and comparative analyses of the limits of economic policies in addressing human-development needs and the role of noneconomic policies in development, the dominant strategies and prescriptions have continued to focus heavily on economic considerations.

Social policies as agents of development

Social-Policy Reform in Comparative Perspective was written to help to close a gap in development research. It examines the role of social policies in promoting development by looking at three countries — Ghana, Chile, and Canada — where governments have experimented with a variety of reform packages to address development objectives. The study is a collective effort to shed greater light on the experiences of these countries in responding to changing human- and social-development concerns at different phases of their economic development and to gain a deeper understanding of the relationship between social policies and social-development outcomes.

This study considers an "integrationist" approach, with its emphasis on the need to simultaneously pursue and integrate economic- and social-development objectives. As the country analyses in this volume confirm, the appropriate mix of social and economic policies to meet broader development goals is neither easy to determine nor easy to implement. Moreover, their successful integration depends heavily on such variables as governance structures, leadership, institutional and policy frameworks, and the international economic and political environment. Their cumulative impact depends, perhaps as importantly, on more practical issues of policy design and implementation.

In contrast to the heavy focus to date on economic policies, this study seeks to draw special attention to the ways governments in Ghana, Chile, and Canada have used social policies, alongside their economic policies, to achieve human-development goals. More specifically, the studies focus on social-reform programs adopted in these countries in response to persistent or emerging development problems, ranging from widespread poverty in Ghana, to a lack of social participation in Chile, to unemployment in Canada.

Social policies are defined in this study as deliberate public strategies to tailor economic growth to serve explicit social objectives and needs. They are by definition culturally and socially specific. Inevitably, as the individual country studies in this volume make abundantly clear, each country has developed its social policies in response to its economic conditions, sociocultural environment, and political regime. Although historically each of these countries has been unique in the particulars and performance of its social-policy framework, they have all given the state a predominant role in providing social services and programs.

As the following chapters illustrate, however, the model of the welfare state in each of its many forms has increasingly come under strain. The failure of the command economies of the Cold War era, the growing influence of international financial institutions and the conditionalities attached to externally driven economic-reform programs, and the impacts of globalization on nation-states' control over their domestic policies have changed the state's role in development. Reform programs in each of the three countries under examination have, for example, included such policy measures as privatizing and decentralizing social services, establishing various eligibility criteria to target social programs, and introducing user fees for social services. Interestingly, these reforms have often been embraced on the grounds that they are expected to maximize public investments and improve the performance of government policies and programs in the social sectors. However, until now, no adequate research had been done on the nature, direction, anticipated benefits, and actual results of the ongoing reforms. In most cases, social-policy reforms have been pursued without sufficient knowledge of the factors that influence their success or failure. The available information tends to be polarized between the competing normative views of mainstream neoliberalism and its critics. Assessments of implementation experiences are required to develop empirically informed policy options. This is one of the challenges that this book attempts to meet.

The choice of Ghana, Chile, and Canada for closer analysis should be explained. These countries are not only radically different but also situated at distant points on any international development scale. For example, Ghana ranked 132nd in the 1997 Human Development Index (HDI) and is a low-income developing country where poverty alleviation has been the key social-policy challenge for successive governments. Critical development indicators in Ghana reveal a life expectancy of 56.6 years, an adult-literacy rate of 63.4%, and a per capita gross national product (GNP) of 390 USD. The country has limited economic capacity, a negative growth rate, and a growing and youthful population with many needs and demands. Historically, Ghana's social policies have been minimalist, largely inadequate, and ineffective. In contrast to Ghana, Chile is a middle-income country with an impressive ranking of 30th in the 1997 HDI. With a per capita GNP of 4 160 USD, the Chilean population has a life expectancy of 75 years and an adult-literacy rate of 95%. Chile's recent economic recovery has frequently been called a miracle, and the Chilean model has been held up for emulation in other countries. Chile has experimented with various development strategies in the last few decades, culminating in its current liberal, free-market economy and its pluralistic political system. Unlike Ghana, Chile has a relatively extensive social-policy infrastructure, which has no doubt contributed significantly to its relatively high standard of living. Finally, Canada is an industrialized country, a member of the Group of Seven and the Organisation for Economic Co-operation and Development (OECD). It has occupied the highest ranking in the HDI in recent years and prides itself in having a well-developed social-policy framework. It is a high-income country, with a GNP per capita of 19 380 USD, a life expectancy of 79 years, and an adult-literacy rate of 99%. Yet, Canada is currently experiencing serious economic and social problems, such as high rates of unemployment, child poverty, a large national debt, and a continuing threat to its unity from a powerful separatist movement in Quebec.

Despite the marked differences among these countries and the fact that each has a distinct social-policy system, it is worth noting that today all three are confronting policy challenges that have led them to redefine their social policies in significant ways. In each case, the new prescriptions for more effective, efficient, and equitable social policies are sought in measures that involve a redefinition of the role of the state in development and that provide for significant innovation in social-policy design and implementation. Thus, the experiences of Ghana, Chile, and Canada may have implications beyond their particular contexts, and these implications may emerge from a comparative study of their reforms.

The case studies in this volume are interpretive essays, rather than in-depth country profiles. In fact, each of the three country-study chapters provides a general trajectory of social policies in a particular setting over time. As social policies are products of concrete socioeconomic conditions and political processes, the authors offer distinctive analyses of the nature, evolution, and operation of social policies in their countries.

The studies in this volume show that the very definition and scope of social policy differs from country to country and within each country over time. As the intent of this volume is primarily to describe how individual countries have defined and implemented policies to deal with nagging social-development concerns, it was considered appropriate to allow the authors the flexibility to determine the scope and boundaries of their analyses within a minimal common framework. Each author was asked to address four common issues:

- The historical and current context for social-policy reforms in the country of study;

- The rationale, principles, and expected outcomes of ongoing reforms;
- The dynamics and institutional underpinnings of the social-policy reforms; and
- Any key issues for further research and analysis that emerged from the historical study of the country's social policies.

These four issues were emphasized not only to highlight the specifics of the experience of the three countries in responding to their unique social-development needs but also to gain a greater appreciation of the importance of the institutional and policy frameworks in developing effective reforms.

Divergent experiences and common themes

It is difficult to draw easy or replicable lessons from the experiences of Ghana, Chile, and Canada in reforming their social-policy systems. However, as the following analyses indicate, the development challenges these three countries have so far faced and will undoubtedly continue to face in new forms in the future demand ongoing policy innovation and reform.

The concluding chapter seeks to situate the country-specific experiments in social-policy reform within the contemporary context of development theory and practice; it considers some limitations of the long-standing debate between the neoliberal school and its critics and reflects on the emerging integrationist perspective on development. Drawing on the experiences of Ghana, Chile, and Canada, as well as from the broader body of literature on social-policy reform, the concluding chapter identifies four critical themes in policy implementation and the related research issues. These themes are useful in comparing the country-specific analyses.

The first concerns the decentralization of social policies. What emerges from the country studies, as well as from other relevant literature, is that a wide range of policy options and a new array of policy actors are involved in current efforts to decentralize social policy. Country-specific approaches to decentralization yield variable outcomes, as a result of important contextual factors, such as institutional capacity, political institutions, and financial resources. Second is the theme of the democratic underpinnings and consequences of social-policy reform, and the concluding chapter points to the contradictory nature of current evidence about the democratizing character and impacts of recent experiments in social-policy reform. Under the third theme, the concluding chapter discusses the privatization of social policies. Once again, the outcomes of different privatization strategies are found to be rooted in a host of normative and operational choices, and this belies any claims that privatization provides an effective solution to overstretched and inefficient public programs; instead, the answers to the relevant questions about the costs and benefits of different privatization schemes should be sought in their particular design and implementation. Finally, the concluding chapter identifies the principles, technical prerequisites and capacities and the financial and operational mechanisms that have informed the various schemes to target social policies; it again draws attention to the wide range of determinants of the social and economic impacts of these schemes.

This volume serves to draw attention to the promise and potential of the comparative study of social policies. We have sufficient evidence to suggest that the current wave of social-policy reforms in both the developing and the industrialized countries is the result of a radical rethinking and major overhaul of some of the basic premises of post-World War II development orthodoxy and that the current wave of social-policy reforms warrants a more rigorous analysis of the variations in social-policy choices and social-development outcomes. Under these circumstances, it is important and legitimate to expect that the comparative study of social policies can only flourish and become a key component of development studies.

Chapter 2

Ghana

Social-policy Reform in Africa

Ernest Aryeetey and Markus Goldstein

Among the most important challenges for social-policy reform in Africa will be to have social services more targeted and sustainable. Social services are usually thought to include health, education, social security, social work, and housing; a wider understanding might encompass a variety of other services, such as sanitation, employment, corrections, and legal services (Spicker 1995). For purposes of comparative study, however, a useful observation is that social policy may have different emphases, depending on the country or region. Although in developed countries, social policy commonly involves public programs directed at a variety of levels and types of social need, in the developing world, they often have a practical focus on poverty alleviation.

In Ghana, the focus is largely on the alleviation of poverty through services to assist the poor to build on their human capital and increase their incomes. Problems of poverty, particularly rural poverty, are a major concern. However, in recent decades, this country has failed to establish a clear and articulated approach to social policy and social-development goals; rather, approaches to social development have tended to be subordinated to more general economic-development strategies and, more recently, shaped by the principles and prescriptions of the Economic Recovery Program (ERP), initiated in 1983. This program is premised on the expectation that the removal of macroeconomic constraints to growth and development can result in more equal opportunities and access to services for all social groups. This laissez-faire approach to social policy means that the social outcomes of reforms generally have not resulted from planned public programs or activities to achieve predetermined social objectives; instead, the often negative outcomes have resulted from the ways various social groups have benefited or failed to benefit from opportunities on the basis of their prereform socioeconomic positions.

This chapter argues that social policy in Ghana in recent years has been subordinated to the imperatives of economic reform and has, as a consequence, been incoherent and residual. This has had important consequences for social development. There is widespread evidence today, more than a decade after reforms began, that expectations for improved equity have not been realized (Norton et al. 1995). With respect to rural poverty-alleviation programs, as well as, more particularly, the dominant sectors of health and education, Ghana's failure to achieve important social-development goals is rooted in various causes, ranging from a lack of policy commitment and necessary resource allocation to an absence of adequate institutional frameworks and effective targeting strategies. The lack of significant targeting in most social programs, as well as the substitution of foreign aid for domestic social spending during the ERP, illustrates the absence of any well-articulated, strategic, or developmental social policy.

This chapter reviews Ghana's approach to social policy, primarily in the context of the country's macroeconomic-reform strategy. It provides a brief review of the dimensions of poverty in Ghana and focuses on the implications of structural-adjustment policies for social policy and social development. It assesses the institutional dimensions of evolving approaches to social policy and reviews the changing roles of central and local governments, the private sector, nongovernmental organizations (NGOs), and donors in the provision of social services and concludes with some reflections on key issues and opportunities for research.

Some dimensions of poverty in Ghana

An overview of social policy in Ghana is appropriately anchored in a certain perspective on its poverty and social-development levels. In the 1980s, the extent of the deprivation suffered by vulnerable groups was outlined in a report of the United Nations Children's Fund (UNICEF 1986). UNICEF presented a picture of severe deterioration in all the key social indicators, arising from increasing poverty, inadequate nutrition, and ineffective social services between the late 1970s and early 1980s. It was estimated that during this decade the proportion of the population below an absolute poverty line rose from around 60-65% to 65-75% in rural areas and from 30-35% to 45-50% in urban areas. This study also showed that the deprivation was significantly worse for people living in those parts of the country that historically had been substantially below the national average for various social indicators. Such areas, including most of northern Ghana and the country's coastal regions, had structural and endemic poverty, difficult environmental conditions, and poor social infrastructure and services.

Following economic reforms, attempts were made in the latter part of the 1980s to capture the effects of broad policy changes on Ghanaian households. The first Ghana Living Standards Survey (GLSS 1) indicated that poverty appeared to have gradually decreased in Ghana during this period, increasing from 36.9% in 1988 to 41.8% in 1989 and then decreasing to 31.4% in 1992 (GSS 1995). In defining poverty, the Ghana Statistical Service (GSS) used relative measures. For the GLSS 1, the upper poverty line was defined as two-thirds of the mean income in 1988, whereas the lower poverty line was half that amount. Despite these figures, however, recent reductions in poverty are considered fragile, and the World Bank (1995a) even suggested that poverty might be on the rise after 1992.

In part, the persistence of poverty in Ghana is related to its rural base. Whereas steady economic growth followed the initiation of reforms in 1983, the agricultural sector continued to perform badly. As 60% of the population depends on agriculture for its livelihood, these difficulties have had wide-ranging implications for poverty. Obsolete production practices, severe resource constraints, and lack of access to information over the years have limited the scale of agricultural activity to very low and, in many instances, subsistence levels. Real incomes are low, and this impairs the ability of rural households to meet their basic needs and make significant contributions to the gross national product.

Recent analysis makes clear not only that poverty levels are regionally oriented but also that they are different for various social groups. In 1993 and 1994, the World Bank coordinated a donor-financed effort to examine poverty, using participatory techniques in 15 communities in 9 of Ghana's 10 regions (Norton et al. 1995). The participatory poverty assessment (PPA) identified a number of poor groups. First, it shed more light on those at the very bottom of the distribution. This group is usually characterized by lack of access to productive assets, especially labour resources, as a result of such factors as widowhood, disability, and age. Second, social networks are also important as buffers against poverty, and the PPA determined that migrant groups in particular tend to have below-average access to social networks. According to a growing body of evidence, however, social networks are rapidly disappearing among nonmigrant populations in urban areas as well. Third, a significant amount of seasonal poverty was found in the rural north, with large portions of the community unable to diversify income sources beyond the single growing season and thus continuing to suffer a lean season. Finally, female headship seems to be associated with poverty in the north but also seems to be linked with other factors, such as the inadequacy of a kin network. Together with more general measures of poverty, then, the survey underscored not only the degree but also the diversity of poverty and social needs of the country. Indeed, the challenges for social policy and social development are underscored by the findings of the 1997 *Human Development Report* (UNDP 1997). Access to safe water and adequate nutrition remains significantly limited; life expectancy stands at 56.6 years; 36.4% of the population is illiterate; and the combined gross enrollment rate is 44%. Overall, current data indicate that Ghana maintains one of the lowest ratings on the United Nations Development Programme's (UNDP's) Human Development Index.

Social policies in the context of economic reform

A historical sketch of social-policy development in Ghana necessarily focuses on strategies for urban but particularly rural development, in addition to more traditional, sector-specific policies and programs. In recent decades, social-development goals and the means of achieving them have been closely linked to broader strategies of economic development. This section briefly reviews development strategies in Ghana in the 1960s and 1970s, argues that the social content of these strategies was weak, and then presents a more detailed discussion of the recent macroeconomic reforms and their implications for social development in Ghana.

Social policy in the 1960s

Following Ghana's independence, in 1957, the main goals of development planning became steady economic growth and improvements in living standards for the urban and rural populations. Although the government focused its attention primarily on economic development and did not articulate a clear set of social-policy objectives, public interventions and expenditure patterns nevertheless suggested some social orientation during this period. There was a sustained upward trend in the social sector's share of government spending in Ghana between 1960 and 1965. Social-sector spending, however, collapsed briefly during the expenditure-cutting years of 1966–68, after Kwame Nkrumah was overthrown.

In the 1960s, the 7-year plan (1963–70) of President Kwame Nkrumah provided the context for Ghana's economic-development strategy. The plan laid the foundation for industrial activity in the country — a strategy consistent with the dominant development philosophies of the time, which emphasized industrialization strategies as the best means of addressing poverty and deprivation. The state assumed a major role in establishing these industries. This appeared to represent a sound approach to economic development; the government expected that rising urban industrial incomes from wage labour in the new industries would stimulate competition that would in turn lead to higher agricultural incomes and improved levels of social well-being.

The Nkrumah government's approach to social development in the 1960s was shaped by the requirements and eventually by the failure of this economic-development strategy. When real wages failed to rise as expected, the government began to emphasize the direct provision of skills for the labour market and building the nation's human capital. These approaches entailed more explicit social interventions. The churches had led earlier campaigns to provide both primary and secondary education, as well as health-care facilities; however, with the evolution of the industrialization strategy and urbanization trends, these efforts were found to be inadequate to meet the needs of the growing mass of people who were leaving agricultural households to seek urban industrial jobs. Thus, the central government directed resources increasingly to secondary and technical education and exhorted local-government bodies to invest in primary and middle schools. Under the plan, it was expected that school enrollment would double in the period of 1963–70 while central government investment in education rose from 5.4 million to 61.3 million GBP (in 1998, 0.6 pounds sterling [GBP] = 1 United States dollar [USD]). The policy of tuition-free education was introduced with the 1961 Education Act. The government considered education a priority for the industrialization strategy and observed that "the stage has now been reached where educational policy must increasingly concern itself with ... the teaching of skills and other attainments that are needed for the running of a modern economy" (GOG 1964, p. 142). Parallel efforts were made to render health care more accessible, particularly through a shift from hospital-based curative medicine to a more preventive, popular approach. Finally, efforts were made to meet the housing needs of the rapidly growing urban population. Indeed, the development plan recognized housing for the urban population as the most pressing need at the time.

Despite these concerted attempts to address basic needs, the Nkrumah government's interventions faltered as financial and human resources diminished through decelerating and, later, negative economic growth. The decline in per capita income also presented a serious challenge for social development. In the 1960s, the majority of people in Ghana had begun to look increasingly to the public sector to provide education and health services; however, this occurred precisely at a time when the state's capacity to provide these services was weakening. Moreover, with the notable exception of the health sector, the focus of social interventions throughout the 1960s was largely on meeting the needs of people in the growing urban areas. However, as the industrialization strategy confronted difficulties the urban problems multiplied and the capacity of the state to address them became substantially overtaxed. In the 1970s, it was therefore not surprising that the government turned its attention to achieving effective rural development.

Social policy in the 1970s

During the 1970s, the development literature became generally dominated by the concept of satisfying the basic needs of poor households and providing them with opportunities for self-enhancement (Streeten 1979). Given that world-wide economic growth in the 1960s did not "trickle-down" to the majority in the Third World, mostly African nations, the need was perceived to attack the problem of poverty more directly. This emphasis led to greater global support for a rural focus in development strategy and planning.

These trends influenced the development strategies in Ghana of the 1970s. In addition to having a new rural focus, the revised rationale was that many of the issues dominating public concern (for example, food, health care, housing, etc.) would only be addressed effectively through efforts at the community level. The prevailing wisdom was that people themselves were capable of creating local solutions to national social and economic problems, and this perspective reinforced the perception that many private and especially public institutions had grown so large that they were no longer efficient or responsive. Indeed, the cost of solving problems in a centralized manner had become prohibitively high. Self-help efforts, with individuals and communities taking greater control over the issues affecting their lives, were considered a more effective and sustainable way of dealing with many of the problems of the poor.

Owing to these influences, in 1970 the government of Prime Minister Kofia Busia (1969–72) embarked on a comprehensive rural-development program, albeit one that placed greater emphasis on infrastructure development than on the provision of social services. A limited expansion of expenditures on health and education was accompanied by a significant investment in economic services, in particular an extensive network of feeder roads linking rural settlements to larger centres, along with an ambitious program for rural electrification and water supply. New health posts and health centres were established, and rural housing projects were begun under the supervision of a new public department. It is generally thought that the Busia government gave most attention to rural development before the 1990s but relatively little clarity in social policy.

As with the earlier push for rapid growth, the new focus on basic needs cut across political barriers and shaped the policies of the military regime that took office in 1972. The new leaders introduced such programs as Operation Feed Yourself (OFY) and Operation Feed the Nation. These were essentially agricultural-development programs to provide both rural and urban households with subsidized planting material, with the intention of doubling food production within a 3-year period. A further major initiative for rural development during this period was the Upper Region Agricultural Development Program (URADEP), initiated in 1975 in consultation with international development agencies. URADEP had as its objective the development of the Upper Region through provision of farm-support services. It was designed to improve rates of agricultural production, but it also had some important social goals, including improved farm incomes and the provision of water and farmer education. The success of these programs was limited, however. The OFY program suffered from poor planning and a tendency to concentrate resources on large commercial farmers and the remaining state farms. Mikell (1991) attributed the failure of the OFY to the declining significance of land as a production constraint as against labour, which had in the meantime become more significant but was not addressed under the OFY policy. Under URADEP, production improvements varied, and by 1981 less than half of the crops had achieved expected increases (Aryeetey 1985). With respect to its impact on social development and social well-being, rural people expressed considerable misgivings about its contribution.

By the end of the 1970s, then, no clear pattern had emerged in Ghana's social policy. Rural development had attracted considerable attention and provided a general framework for public approaches to social development. Moreover, if the state machinery and public expenditure on social services had grown in the 1970s (rising to 46% of the total budget in fiscal year 1976/77), then the end of the decade saw a return to more modest levels. By 1981, expenditures on social sectors constituted only 33% of total spending (ISSER 1996). Ghana was also under increasing pressure to undertake economic reform and more effective and efficient resource allocation (Table 1).

The Economic Recovery Program: social policy and economic reform from 1983 to the present

With the advent, in 1981, of the military regime under Jerry Rawlings, the economic performance of Ghana showed a range of negative trends. These included weak growth in agriculture and industry; poor

Table 1. Central-government expenditure on social services, Ghana, 1957–96.

	1957–66	1967–71	1972–82	1983–91	1992–96
Central-government expenditure as a share of GDP by sector (narrow coverage)					
Public services	5.4	6.0	4.3	2.9	2.5
Economic services	10.6	6.8	7.0	8.1	10.9
Agriculture	2.0	1.4	1.6	0.6	0.3
Infrastructure	8.3	5.2	5.4	7.1	9.9
Roads	4.8	3.9	4.8	6.8	9.6
Transport, storage, and communication	1.9	1.0	0.3	0.2	0.1
Power and electricity	1.1	0.1	0.0	0.0	0.1
Water and sanitation	0.5	0.5	0.3	0.1	0.1
Other economic services	0.3	0.2	0.0	0.4	0.8
Social services	6.1	6.9	6.4	5.2	6.0
Education	3.7	4.2	3.6	3.0	4.4
Health	1.3	1.4	1.3	1.2	1.3
Other social expenditures	1.1	1.4	1.5	1.1	0.3
Central-government expenditure as a share of total expenditures and net lending by sector (narrow coverage)					
Public services	22.3	28.1	22.9	23.0	20.7
Economic services	29.0	17.1	16.9	17.1	15.8
Agriculture	8.4	6.4	9.1	4.7	1.3
Infrastructure	19.4	10.4	7.6	9.5	10.8
Roads and waterways	4.8	3.9	4.8	6.8	9.6
Transport, storage, and communication	8.1	4.6	1.6	1.9	0.3
Power and electricity	4.2	0.6	0.2	0.2	0.4
Water and sanitation	2.3	1.3	1.1	0.6	0.5
Other economic services	1.2	1.2	0.2	2.9	3.6
Social services	25.2	32.2	33.8	39.9	32.1
Education	15.3	19.6	19.1	22.9	20.3
Health	5.2	6.3	7.0	8.7	6.2
Other social expenditures	4.7	6.2	7.7	8.3	5.6

Source: Central Bureau of Statistics, *Statistical Yearbook, 1967–68*, *Quarterly Digest of Statistics*, various years, and World Bank data.

Note: *Quarterly Digest of Statistics* data through 1987 are broken down into General Administration, Defence, and Justice and Police. Data from 1987 are broken down as Foreign Affairs, Interior and Defence, and Other Government. Categories do not add to 100 because of unallocable expenditures, which include transfers to local governments, interest payments on public debt, and other and are not shown. GDP, gross domestic product.

export performance, following low commodity prices; mounting debt within an unfavourable trade climate; worsening social conditions, as a result of food insecurity; inadequate housing; and rising unemployment. These problems were exacerbated by large fiscal deficits, financed primarily by borrowing from the domestic banks, which in turn gave rise to high rates of inflation and an overvalued currency. Government intervention in the economy, as well as massive expansion of the public sector through an increasing number of state enterprises, had produced distortions in the economy and destroyed incentives to save and invest. The severe shortage of foreign exchange and imported goods led to a deterioration of services and a decline in capital investments. As domestic resources shrank the demand for foreign assistance grew significantly.

The economic crisis in Ghana prompted the introduction of the ERP in 1983. The ERP was based on the principles of structural adjustment and emphasized the liberalization of the economy and less dependence on the public sector for the delivery of goods and services; in other words, it emphasized a "small" state. It also placed emphasis on the gradual liberalization of the exchange rate and trade system to improve resource allocation and the external-payments position.

The ERP had important implications, both in principle and in practice, for approaches to social policy in Ghana. Two features of the program were particularly significant: first, macroeconomic considerations overrode many others, including specific or strategic commitments to social-development goals; second (and in part this is an explanation for the first feature), the ERP was based on the philosophy that continuous growth, following liberalization policies, would eventually or somehow inevitably lead to a more equitable social distribution. Moreover, reinforcing this noninterventionist ideological orientation was a nonparticipatory political process. In Ghana, it can be argued that the failure of the ERP to respond adequately to the essential social needs of the Ghanaian population was in part due to a limited local sense of ownership of the program and control over its design and implementation.

Indeed, considerable discussion has taken place about whether even the Ghanaian government owned the reform program and how such ownership or the lack of it affected its social-development programs (Aryeetey 1995). Although the government has always maintained that the reform program was a domestic response to the country's economic situation, others have contended that a dearth of local technical capacity prohibited an appropriate or effective national response (Toye 1991). Still others have contended that a reliance on the International Monetary Fund and the World Bank was dictated by a number of factors, including the failure of Ghana to secure aid from most bilateral sources. Certainly, for its part, the World Bank's assessment of reform ownership (Johnson and Wasty 1993) placed particular emphasis on the commitment of the leadership in Ghana and less on the locus of initiative. Concerned primarily with the commitment of Ghana's leadership to reforms, the Bretton Woods Institutions did little to encourage the government to consult other institutions, not even the universities, the private sector, or trade unions. Proponents of the ERP within the Ghanaian government were fully aware of, and persuaded by, the need to conform to the Washington consensus on the need to achieve macroeconomic stability ahead of other goals, including those of social development. In this context, lack of consultation may be used as a yardstick to measure the degree of Ghanaian ownership. Here we note that the Rawlings government carried out a massive program to reform the education sector while citing the need to accommodate World Bank conditionalities and schedules for disbursements as the major reason for its intolerance of extensive discussion.

The ERP was generally expected to have serious consequences for social spending in Ghana. The expected fall in budgetary allocations to the social sectors under the ERP elicited some opposition. Resistance was largely expected to come from urban workers, who were considered the primary beneficiaries of a system of subsidies for social services and deliberate controls on agricultural pricing. For organized labour, reducing the fiscal deficit through the removal of subsidies and through the implementation of measures to improve cost-effectiveness in the delivery of social services was a major fear, right from the beginning of reforms. Left-wing groups mounted significant opposition to cuts. Because adjustment burdens were expected to fall disproportionately on the poor, opponents argued particularly for exemptions and other forms of targeting. However, the Rawlings government remained committed to a neoliberal reform strategy in the perceived lack of credible or feasible alternatives from the Left.

During the early years of the economic reforms, however, social spending as a share of total government spending actually increased from a low level of 31% in 1983 to a high of 46% in 1990. It also increased its share in gross domestic product (GDP). However, much of this increase was sustained by significant increases in donor flows, especially to the social sectors (Table 2). By 1991, donor contributions to social spending reached 34.6% of the total. After 1990, this trend was reversed, and as aid declined the government's spending on social sectors fell sharply (Figure 1; see Table 1). In 1995, social-sector spending was only 36% of the total budget, and decreases were recorded for spending on health, education, social security, and welfare.

In combination with the decline in foreign aid, a key reason for the declining shares of the social sector in public spending in the 1990s was the crowding out of social spending by public-sector interest payments under economic adjustment. The share of interest payments doubled between 1990 and 1994, from 10% to 20% of the total

Table 2. Aid and spending on social-sector development, Ghana, 1988–93.

	1988	1989	1990	1991	1992	1993
Social-sector ODA–GDP (%)	0.5	0.7	0.9	2.0	1.6	1.7
Social-sector ODA–government social expenditure (%)	7.1	10.2	14.4	34.6	22.9	21.2

Source: UNDP (1993a) and CSO (1991, 1994).
Note: GDP, gross domestic product; ODA, overseas development assistance.

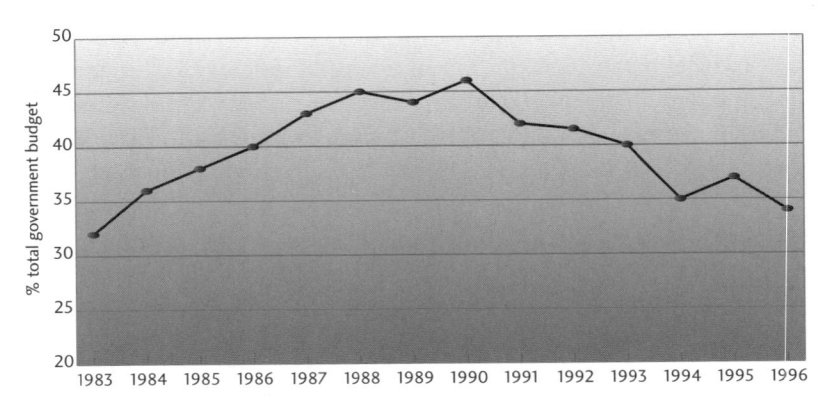

Figure 1. Community and social-service spending.

budget. Social-sector spending in particular in the last few years has been affected by the rise in interest payments as the share of spending on economic services has been maintained (ISSER 1996). An additional explanation for social-spending cuts, as well as for their distribution, may also be political. With the reintroduction of a democratic system of governance, many Ghanaians believe that in places where reductions in public spending have been called for, the government has become interested in ensuring more visible services, such as roads and electricity, in hopes of a political windfall. In places where rural populations are considered the principal backers of the government, it seems politicians have accurately perceived the provision of infrastructure to be more politically useful than alternative potential investments in health and education services. Thus, as the government has come under pressure from within and from without to reduce the current fiscal deficit of more than 8% of GDP and to meet macroeconomic targets, it has been easier for it to argue for a cut in these social services and switch the available development resources to roads, which donors would be unlikely to fund.

In placing emphasis on macroeconomic stability and commitments to a minimal state and conservative fiscal management, the ERP has generally entailed a relatively laissez-faire or ad hoc approach to social policy and development in Ghana. As we suggest below, attempts to address the social costs of the ERP have been compensatory and poorly managed; revised approaches to key social sectors, particularly health and education, have reflected an overriding concern with efficiency, cost-effectiveness, and cost recovery. The ERP has given little attention to questions of equity or the effective targeting of resources to vulnerable groups. In the following, we look briefly at Ghana's efforts to address some of the social costs of adjustment and, in greater detail, at some of the most important changes to its health and education sectors.

Program of Action to Mitigate the Social Costs of Adjustment

The Program of Action to Mitigate the Social Costs of Adjustment (PAMSCAD) was undertaken as a major intersectoral initiative to respond to the social costs of the ERP, and it provides a good example of an ad hoc and poorly designed approach to social needs under the reforms. In February 1988, donors pledged a total of 85.7 million USD to fund 23 projects under its umbrella. Entailing collaboration between donors, district governments, and communities, PAMSCAD comprised many projects, including a range of community initiatives; education, employment, and income-generation projects; and specific assistance for retrenched civil servants.

However, PAMSCAD was plagued by problems from the start. Mid-term and final reviews of the program cited a variety of obstacles to its success, ranging from the slow disbursement of funds by donors to PAMSCAD's overreliance on existing institutions, which in many cases possessed inadequate capacity to meet the demands of the initiative. Thus, for example, a project designed to improve child nutrition faltered because of the infrastructural limitations of local schools (for example, lack of kitchen facilities, dilapidated regional food depots). Similarly, a project to improve local building materials failed because of the weakness of local markets. As one review of PAMSCAD explained, "there was a clear mismatch between expected project outputs and the ability of implementing agencies in terms of manpower available (both skills and number) and other inputs" (Kwadzo and Kumekpor 1994, p. 4). This view of PAMSCAD emphasized the need to include complementary capacity-building strategies.

A further difficulty with the program was found in its implementation and targeting practices. In a review of PAMSCAD, Kwadzo and Kumekpor found that in some cases parents withdrew their children from a supplementary feeding program because of the fees. Kwadzo and Kumekpor also found fault in PAMSCAD's reliance on counterpart contributions, which essentially required up-front investments from poor groups as a prerequisite for their participation. As Kwadzo and Kumekpor (1994, p. 12) observed,

> to expect these same [poor] groups to contribute substantial amount[s of money] to implement the projects in addition to their labor input defeats the objective of PAMSCAD. Similarly, without accurately estimating the cost of projects taking into consideration differences in socio-economic status, skills, natural and environmental conditions, flat amounts were established as assistance for each project in all locations. This was found to be inappropriate and to have contributed to the failure to complete most projects started. To even request that projects must be 60–75% completed to benefit from PAMSCAD assistance from those considered poor and vulnerable was unfortunate since by definition they are vulnerable because they are not capable of helping themselves.

Similar problems with targeting of vulnerable groups were evident in other parts of the program. A project to improve local building materials also highlighted the problem of assuming that markets could be easily developed. Kwadzo and Kumekpor asserted that "the absence of an effective market in the vulnerable areas is due to the subsistence level of existence of the people" and that "special consideration [for] those segments of the population living below subsistence level to benefit from the programs through some form of subsidy is necessary" (Kwadzo and Kumekpor 1994, pp. 35–36). How such targeting was to be accomplished they did not discuss.

Not all components of PAMSCAD failed. The Enhancing Opportunities for Women in Development (ENOWID) project was effectively implemented by an adequately remunerated staff, leading Kwadzo and Kumekpor to call for its extension. ENOWID also enjoyed substantial donor support. The water and sanitation component of PAMSCAD was reasonably successful, delivering a significant number of facilities, as well as education and awareness.

Overall, however, in both its design and implementation, PAMSCAD failed to adequately address the social costs of the ERP. Moreover, its effectiveness was undermined by a range of obstacles, not the least of which was the inability of a number of its projects to ensure participation by the most vulnerable groups and to target resources to them. In numerous instances, communities were expected to initiate projects before assistance was given, with the result that the poorest groups were excluded from participation, services, and benefits. Indeed, PAMSCAD's failures in this regard mirror difficulties with targeting that plague social policy in Ghana more broadly, particularly in the health and education sectors, as discussed below.

Health-sector reforms

The ERP has had important implications for the mainstream, or traditional, social sectors in Ghana. The impact of the ERP on the health sector has been serious. Spending in health has mirrored social-policy spending more generally: government commitments have waned with the reduction of donor support. In 1983, 4.4% of the government budget was devoted to health. This jumped to 8.5% in 1984 and increased to 10.1% in 1989/90. But in the early 1990s, it started to fall, and it was down to 6% by 1995 (ISSER 1994, 1996). Currently, government spending on health is relatively low. Indeed, the government is not the biggest spender on health: private spending constitutes some 51% of the total; the government provides only 37%; and NGOs cover 12% (Demery et al. 1995). Notably, from 1990 to 1994, Ghana's spending on health averaged 1.2% of GDP, whereas the average was 2% for all developing countries (World Bank 1995a).

Specific or effective efforts to target the poor have not been part of the reform strategy in Ghana. In health, as in other sectors, budget streamlining and cost-effectiveness have been the governing principles of restructuring. One important dimension of the reforms in health care is the imposition of fees for health services. As far back as 1971, the government collected user fees as a means to increase cost recovery in this sector. The fees were kept low until 1985, when they increased sharply under the ERP, and patients were expected to pay for everything except vaccinations and treatment for some diseases. Following the increases, however, fees were not regularly adjusted and their contribution to the budget of the Ministry of Health steadily declined. Moreover, not only is it recognized that the introduction of user charges has limited access to health facilities in the last decade, but also there is growing concern that health services are deteriorating rapidly, which makes it difficult to justify the payment of fees.

Problems with the health-care reforms do not relate exclusively to cost-recovery measures, however. A further problem stems from the intrasectoral allocation of resources. By 1986, as much as 75% of the Ministry of Health's recurrent budget went to the payment of wages and salaries, which climbed from 44% in 1978. The cutback on other goods and services implied by this pattern has severely constrained primary health care at the community level by restricting the mobile health units, field supervision, and deliveries of essential supplies (Kwapong et al. 1996). Still other problems arise from the health system's becoming increasingly inequitable. Poor links between public and private health facilities have led to an underuse of available health resources. An estimated 50% of medical practitioners in Ghana are in private practice, and no incentives are offered to encourage them to expand their outreach to rural areas (Kwapong et al. 1996). Finally, some logistical deficiencies have had important consequences for access. Health-service delivery in Ghana continues to be institution based, granting only 65% of the population access to facilities. On average, people have to travel 12 km to reach a health centre and 40 km to reach a hospital.

The limited allocation of resources to the health sector and the means by which resources are managed and distributed within this sector clearly have important consequences for equitable social development. Under the ERP, health-sector reforms are generally perceived to have had few positive impacts on beneficiaries. Indeed, Demery et al.'s (1995) analysis of intrasectoral spending confirmed that the situation was inequitable and that resources were not being directed to the most vulnerable groups. Using a technique that matches use by different groups, as well as distribution of spending, they estimated the average incidence of public spending. With some qualifications, their results showed a significantly regressive spending regime. In 1989, the poorest quintile in Ghana received only 12.2% of total government health spending, whereas the top quintile received 30.4%. In 1992, the distribution had worsened somewhat, as the bottom quintile captured 11.6% of spending and the top quintile captured 33%. Disaggregating this distribution by gender for the 1992 data also yielded some disturbing patterns. Although women as a whole commanded a larger share of health expenditure (56.2%, compared with the men's 43.8%), this pattern was not found among the poorest quintile. Indeed, in that quintile, women garnered only 44.3% of spending on health. In contrast, women in the top quintile got 65% of spending on health. All in all, these results are worrying because, when the caveats to the study are considered, the actual picture is worse.

There are a number of caveats. First, because the Ministry of Health did not provide sufficient disaggregation, figures were for the Greater Accra, Eastern, Volta, Ashanti, and Western regions only. Second, because of the structure of the GLSS, data on in-patient care were severely underestimated, leading the results to underestimate the regressive nature of spending. Finally, one should keep in mind the point made above — that the poor are less likely to report an illness and to seek treatment in general. We should note that Demery et al. also found low use of the health system — about half of the people who reported sick in 1992 did not seek treatment.

Given the consequences of the ERP for health, then, it is not surprising that more than a decade after this reform began, the public outcry has continued to grow. Steady calls persist from the public for the government to discontinue the "cash-and-carry" system that ensures that patients at many facilities receive treatment and medication only after satisfying financial obligations. Kwapong et al. (1996) suggested that the health system still had serious shortcomings, including the following:

- People cannot access the health care they need, in either the rural or urban areas;
- The quantity and quality of services are far less than users demand;
- Scarce resources are used inefficiently;
- There are weak linkages between the public and private delivery mechanisms, as well as between the centre and the health facilities in small communities; and
- The health sector is underfunded, as a per capita expenditure of only 6 USD is allocated to the Ministry of Health, which is a drop from 10 USD in 1978.

These trends notwithstanding, some recent progress was made in health care in Ghana. Per 1 000 live births, infant mortality in 1994 was 66.4, and the figure for children under 5 years of age was 119.4. Both these figures were better than the average for sub-Saharan Africa. Within Ghana, however, there were large variations in these rates by region.

Education-sector reforms

As in the health sector, the economic decline and the ERP have had important impacts on the education sector in Ghana. Again, during the economic decline of the 1970s and early 1980s, education provision suffered drastically. Spending per primary-school pupil fell from 41 USD in 1975 to 16 USD in 1983 (Demery et al. 1995). In gauging the incidence of education spending, Demery et al.'s data were of a better quality than those for health. The researchers gave two caveats, however. First, the absence of data on cost recovery left them with estimates of gross distribution only. Second, the absence of regional data precluded the differentiation of costs by region and hence resulted in some loss of variation. In the 1980s, commitments to education moved in tandem with those to other social sectors, rising to 25.3% of the national budget. Once again, however, during the 1990s, the gains evaporated, and spending dropped below the levels of the early 1980s (ISSER 1994, 1996).

By contrast with patterns in health, those of spending distribution in education are relatively more equitable. In 1989, the bottom quintile received 17.1% and the top quintile 23.7%. By 1992, both groups had lost part of their shares to the middle quintiles. When these data were broken down by type of education, different patterns emerged. The distribution of spending on primary education was quite equitable, with the bottom three quintiles capturing more than 20% of expenditures. Furthermore, the share of the lowest quintile improved marginally in the 1989-92 period. Tertiary education (with only 12% of the education-sector budget) showed the opposite effect. Here the bottom two quintiles, 40% of the population, only accounted for 16% of total spending. The top quintile alone, on the other hand, accounted for 45% in 1992. Demery et al. (1995) also gave evidence of a persistent gender bias in education spending. Girls in the bottom quintile got only 40.6% of that quintile's education spending. Girls in the top quintile did not fare much better, capturing 44.5% of that quintile's share. Similarly, positive trends were related to enrollment rates, which have increased in recent years. Net enrollment in primary schools rose from 62% in 1987/88 to 74% in 1991/92. Although enrollment in secondary schools was far below expected, net enrollment at this level nevertheless rose to 38% in 1991/92 from 32% in 1987/88 (GSS 1995).

Geographic disparities in education in 1996 were also striking. Rural-urban distinctions showed a significant discrepancy. Whereas the national enrollment rate in primary school was 67.4%, the rural-only enrollment rate was 54%. Regional breakdowns revealed a 66.6% attendance rate in the Greater Accra region; 28.6%, in Upper East region; and 29.8%, in Upper West region (ISSER 1996). The patterns in outcomes were similar. More than half of the overall population (51.2%) was illiterate. This was concentrated in rural areas, where some 60% of the population was completely illiterate. There was, moreover, a very sharp gender division. The male illiteracy rate was 39.2% (for the entire country), and the female illiteracy rate was 61.5% (ISSER 1996).

Despite some positive trends, there is a widespread perception that the educational system in Ghana is not performing up to expectations. Many people hold the view that the government is underinvesting in this sector (Kwapong et al. 1996). Although the current proportion of public expenditure in education is recognized to be relatively large, the absolute amounts are certainly inadequate to achieve the goals set for the transformation of the educational system and educating the growing number of people.

In fact, the challenges currently facing the sector, along with its role in social development, are significant. Inadequately trained staff, insufficient textbooks and classroom furniture, and similar factors all contribute to questionable educational quality – a consequence confirmed by poor performance of graduates on standardized aptitude tests (Glewwe and Jacoby 1992). Further, as in health, rising costs are an issue. The costs associated with a child in school beyond tuition – uniform, books, travel, tariffs for structural works, parent-teacher-association fees, etc. – all add up to a substantial expense, previously covered, in large part, by subsidies. We need to note that quite a number of these expenses were covered under earlier subsidies. As in health, there are problems in education relating to equitable access and the failure to direct adequate resources to the poorest groups. Norton et al. (1995) indicated that the cost of various incidentals are seen by many rural households as a major barrier to health and education. In addition, reforms are perceived to have encouraged the development of an inequitable school system in Ghana, which ensures that the children of the poor attend poorly equipped state schools. Moreover, rural-urban disparities in access compound this situation, with the result that desirable learning outcomes have only been recorded in private and public schools located in large towns and cities, in sharp contrast to the low learning outcomes recorded in the majority of public schools in rural and other deprived areas. Also notable is an uneven distribution of qualified teachers across the country, with cities and large towns getting a disproportionately large share of qualified teachers.

In 1987, the government embarked on radical education-sector reforms at the pretertiary level, with a view to addressing many of these issues. Among the central objectives of the reforms were to improve equitable access, establish investment and resource-management systems, increase the relevance of curricula, and improve performance relating to efficiency and cost recovery. Specifically, the reform program sought to

- Expand and create more equitable access at all levels of education;
- Change the structure of the school system by reducing the length of pretertiary education from 17 years to 12 years and increasing the contact hours between teachers and pupils;
- Improve pedagogic efficiency and effectiveness;
- Ensure that more attention is paid to problem solving, environmental concerns, prevocational training, and manual dexterity;
- Contain and partially recover costs; and
- Enhance sector management and budgeting procedures.

However, recent evaluations of the outcome of the reform program suggested limited success, as is evident from the persistent deficiencies described above. It is generally acknowledged that restructuring the educational system to deliver planned outputs will require significant new investments, recurrent outlays, and more concerted and effective attention to the relationship between education and the achievement of sustainable and equitable social-development goals.

In summary, then, the ERP has not provided an ideology or practical strategy for achieving social-development goals in Ghana. With economic goals and market principles given priority, approaches to social policy and commitments to achieving social-development goals have been secondary at best. Efforts have been directed at measures to render aggregate social-service delivery more cost-effective, rather than more targeted and more equitable. Although reformers initially argued that proper targeting of limited social expenditures would ensure that social services would still benefit the genuinely poor, our review suggests a general failure to deliver on this promise.

The institutional dimensions of social-policy reform

As noted above, underpinning the ERP and macroeconomic reform in Ghana is a commitment to the notion of a relatively small state. The rationale for this approach can be considered at least twofold. First, proponents of neoliberal reform point to the ways significant state involvement in the economy is connected with market distortions, inefficiencies of resource allocation, and failing competitiveness. Second, a prominent role for the state — and, more specifically, the central government — in the economic and social realms is perceived to render public policies and programs, which might otherwise function more optimally, less responsive and less efficient.

In 1992, constitutional requirements enjoined the government of Ghana to establish a long-term program to address various issues of social and economic development. The National Coordinated Program for Social and Economic Development, or Ghana Vision 2020, was the result, and this was intended to be the authoritative government document to guide development across all the major sectors. The stages outlined in Ghana Vision 2020 are divided into two main periods: in the medium term (1996–2000), the development objective is to consolidate the gains achieved under the ERP and strengthen the foundations for accelerated growth; in the long term (1996–2020), the aim is to improve the social and economic status of all individuals and to eliminate extremes of deprivation by encouraging the creativity, enterprise, and productivity of all citizens.

The development objectives contained in Ghana Vision 2020 have been used by the Ministry of Local Government and Rural Development to prepare a National Action Plan for Poverty Reduction (NAPPR). The long-term human-development objective of the NAPPR remains that of improving the quality of life and expanding opportunities for society as a whole, but this is expected to be achieved through the following medium-term steps:

- Alleviating poverty through an improvement of the access of the poor to basic social and technical infrastructure, economic services, and improved participation in decision-making;

- Enhancing human resources through programs on population, women in development, health and nutrition, etc.; and

- Increasing employment and leisure opportunities through the promotion of labour intensive programs, support for the informal sector, and safeguarding of the rights of rural women.

In support of our contention that there remains no commitment or strategic attention to social policy in Ghana, however, it should be noted that the NAPPR is not regarded as a meaningful document by many government agencies, and donors generally disregard it. The government, however, has not denounced it, which is in keeping with the general pattern with respect to similar documents bearing on social policy in the last decade. Such policy documents tend to be cited by interested public-sector agencies whenever convenient to indicate that there is a policy, but in fact these documents carry no significant weight.

One major difficulty with Ghana Vision 2020 as a strategy for social development or poverty alleviation is the absence of significant procedures for targeting or reaching distinct social groups, which is, as we have already suggested, a persistent failing of the government's approach to social development. Once again, the way in which particular social groups will be reached is taken for granted, rather than addressed effectively or systematically under the plan. In addition, however, in the 1990s many of the challenges confronting the government in the social realm relate to changes in the institutional frameworks to achieve social-development goals. Under the ERP, Ghana Vision 2020 or any other development plan is likely to be influenced by a persistent ideological commitment to small central government and to the devolution of responsibility for development to other groups. Under its neoliberal reform strategy, the state seeks to reduce considerably its role in the provision of social services and to promote a greater role for other actors, specifically, local government, the private sector, NGOs, and donors. The following will review some important changes to institutional arrangements for social policy in the country and consider the implications of these shifts for the achievement of social-development goals.

Local governments and communities in social policy

In the last decade, the term decentralization has undoubtedly been one of the most often used by Ghanaian politicians, and most often the emphasis has been on the link between decentralization and "self-reliant" development. Under the ERP, the message has been that local groups and populations will have to bear a greater responsibility for whatever development projects take place in their settlements or districts. The current interest in Ghana in the relationship between the centre and places that depend on it for socioeconomic development follows a trend that was common in many developing countries throughout the 1980s. Many countries have attempted in one way or the other to decentralize their service-delivery systems, albeit with widely varying degrees of success (Conyers 1983).

Since 1988, when the ERP began, Ghana has pursued a decentralized local-government system to ensure that local communities are better provided with social services. New local-government and planning laws enacted after 1989 have emphasized the administrative district as the focal point of planning. Responsibility for the preparation of a national-development plan lies with the National Development Planning Commission (NDPC), but responsibility for subnational development planning is vested in district assemblies operating through their executive committees and a District Planning Coordinating Unit (DPCU). District assemblies are now responsible for preparing and submitting a development plan and budget to central government.

Although in Ghana as elsewhere in the developing world, decentralization has increasingly been regarded as an appropriate strategy for service design and delivery, support for it has been grounded in the important and often untested assumption that key prerequisites for its success are met. For example, in the classical sense, "decentralization is taken to mean the sharing of part of the governmental power by a central ruling group with other groups, each having authority within a specific area of the state" (Illy 1985). In short, it is a conceptualization that presupposes the existence of formal political structures representing local interests, as well as representing the interests of the central ruling group. However, as Subramaniam (1980) noted, because such democratic institutions cannot be assumed to exist in the South, we are forced to approach this concept with caution.

Moreover, if decentralization in the developing world cannot always be assumed to rely on democratic policy-making and planning, the weakness of local institutions poses still other challenges. Cheema and Rondinelli (1983, p. 64) defined decentralization as "the transfer of planning, decision-making, or administrative authority from central government to field organizations, local administrative units, semi-autonomous and para-statal organizations, local governments or non-governmental organizations." Again, mainstream definitions of decentralization presuppose or, at least, emphasize the importance of functional institutional frameworks. Where the capacity of local institutions to assume such new responsibilities is limited, however, as in many parts of the developing world, there may be obstacles to effective decentralization.

In Ghana, the NDPC acts as a central coordinating unit for decentralized planning. Its task is mainly to guide the central government on national-development goals, based on information provided by the district and regional agencies reporting to it. The NDPC prepares comprehensive plans aimed at integrating and harmonizing all subnational (district) and sectoral policies and providing guidelines for all budgetary, price, income, foreign-trade, and human-resource policies. It also has responsibility for synthesizing all policy proposals into an integrated framework for national economic and social development. NDPC is charged with ensuring that district plans do not contradict national goals, but the actual implementation of development plans for specific areas is the responsibility of the district assemblies and their DPCUs.

A major achievement of these decentralization efforts has been the high level of awareness created among local officials of the importance of planning and the requirements for it. Training workshops, awareness programs, and seminars for district administrative staff and other personnel have helped to achieve this appreciable degree of awareness (UNDP 1993a). Moreover, in addition to understanding what decentralized planning is about, local communities are increasingly becoming aware of the importance of self-reliance in development planning in their areas. Some district assemblies currently focus on planning activities and seek financial assistance from sources other than the central government for their programs.

Notwithstanding these positive developments, however, the challenges associated with effective decentralization in Ghana are significant. One major constraint on the provision of social services by local-government bodies is inadequate financial resources. The central government's only contribution has followed from its constitutional obligation to distribute 5% of the development budget among the 110 district assemblies. These amounts are relatively limited. Moreover, even where such resources are transferred, it has been difficult to account for these funds (Kwapong et al. 1996). Cases of misappropriation in various districts have undermined service provision and may in large part be traced to problems with management systems and inadequately trained staff.

Still further difficulties arise from the inadequacy of the systems in place for resource generation at local levels. District assemblies are responsible for harnessing a large part of the resources needed to achieve their development objectives. However, unequal competition with central government renders them practically powerless in the mobilization of resources. For example, although the local governments are empowered by law to levy monies from a number of sources, these are unlikely to yield substantial revenues. These sources of revenue include entertainment duty, casino revenue, betting tax, gambling tax, and income tax (registration of trade, business, profession, or vocation). Other sources of revenue include such fees as market dues, graveyard receipts, licences such as those imposed on beer and wine sellers and hawkers, and miscellaneous other sources, which include court fees and fines, hearse-hiring charges, and stool-land revenue. It has been projected that, from these sources, the average assembly will realize no more than 2% of its annual development expenditure.

In addition to inadequate devolution of financial resources, some difficulties have been related to the reassignment of power and responsibilities. For example, through the decentralization process in Ghana, Regional Coordinating Councils and Regional Planning Coordinating Units have been placed between the NDPC and local district assemblies. Although they are intended to play an intermediary role, these regional bodies possess ambiguous planning functions, with no clear decision-making authority. Given that decentralized planning is essentially about ensuring the capacity and authority to make decisions at lower levels without having to refer to the centre, this failure to clearly define institutional responsibilities, powers, and lines of accountability represents an obstacle to the effective implementation of the process.

A final set of difficulties relates to some embedded assumptions of the decentralization strategies concerning local-level institutional and individual capacities. As noted above, a tendency in Ghana is to assume that the decentralized provision of services automatically renders projects sustainable. However, communities are not always able to assume the roles expected of them. The study by Norton et al. (1995)

demonstrated clearly that although many communities are willing and anxious to participate in the management of social services, their inadequate preparedness for the task (often as a result of poverty and poor management and technical skills), usually creates problems in the implementation of social programs. For example, water and sanitation committees were set up in a number of communities to help manage facilities. They have had little impact on community involvement in financing water projects. Moreover, as the experience of PAMSCAD made clear, the mechanisms by which responsibilities are shifted to local governments and particularly to communities are critical. As we have seen, PAMSCAD's success depended on, and assumed the potential for, local-level initiative and capacity; however, a major problem was that those communities without the necessary resources were summarily excluded. Even in-kind contributions can be draining, especially if there are recurrent labour demands. In addition, project demands for communal labour can run afoul of public-goods issues. Indeed, the PAMSCAD review noted that "the collective activity approach to providing community facilities, though commendable, did not prove fruitful under PAMSCAD. Rather, individualistic tendencies of human nature gave full expression in various projects" (Kwadzo and Kumekpor 1994, p. 7).

The private sector and social policy

The private sector in Ghana has had relatively little to do with social policy or its reform. However, this situation is evolving. In health and education and primarily with a focus on groups other than the poor, the private sector has participated in the provision of social services. In health, we noted that more than 50% of doctors are in the private sector, running small clinics. The interesting thing about this private involvement in health delivery is that it is almost entirely urban based, concentrated in the two largest cities, Accra and Kumasi. Private clinics serve mainly the better-off sections of urban society, which do not want to suffer the inconvenience of poor public services. The state has little involvement in the organization of private clinics, except to set regulations and standards. For education, the situation is not much better. Private basic-education facilities are known to be the best in the country, but they are again largely found in Accra and Kumasi. Kwapong et al. (1996) described the tendency of most senior public officials to place their wards in these schools as an indictment of the publicly owned basic-education facilities. Interestingly, privately owned secondary-school facilities do not have the same reputation. It is recognized that they offer a poorer quality of education than those institutions owned by the state. This is largely related to the fact that the private sector is seldom in a position to raise the resources required to provide good-quality secondary education, including sound infrastructure and adequate remuneration of staff. We must point out that, in the past (particularly in the 1960s), people tended to react negatively to the participation of the private sector in the provision of education. It was generally considered exploitative of the poor and a reflection of a weak state. The perception is only gradually changing.

Most of the provision of housing in both the rural and the urban areas has been private (that is, more than 95%) because the state has usually not considered this sector a priority. Without a housing market, most provision is the responsibility of the users themselves. Most Ghanaians have some stake in the houses they occupy. And the high levels of poverty all over the country make housing quality generally low, particularly in rural areas.

Currently, a discussion is taking place between the Ghanaian government and various donors about strategies to elicit private-sector participation in the provision of a wider set of social and rural services. Specific areas under discussion have included waste management, road construction, and rural water provision and electrification. The driving force behind these initiatives appears to have been a desire to reduce public expenditures and improve efficiency. The little debate that has occurred about the privatization of services has focused on possible inequities in distribution. The main obstacle to greater private-sector participation in social-service delivery appears to be the inability of the sector to make the necessary investment. The considerable public support required for this often leads to questions of private versus social costs and benefits, which Ghanaians have not even begun to answer.

NGOs and social policy

The number of NGOs participating actively in social-service delivery in Ghana has greatly increased, both locally and internationally, in the last decade, especially at the rural-community level. Several of these NGOs are sectarian and receive support from parent organizations in

Europe and the United States. Programs supported by NGOs in general do not differ considerably from government projects, except in scale. NGOs tend to provide support related to welfare programs and relief aid, skills training, credit assistance, and institution-building. These agencies tend to focus on one or two of these areas, but it is not uncommon to find some that support several of them. In rural areas, NGOs often direct resources to water, sanitation, and other health and education programs. In urban areas, their activities for poverty alleviation have been directed at developing welfare programs and strengthening social safety nets. For welfare services, churches in particular have a very good network of contacts with low-income groups, through the parish system. Church development initiatives tend, therefore, to be largely decentralized and designed to meet the needs of the local community. Initially, church projects discriminated against nonmembers, but participation in many of their activities is now often open to nonmembers. The Roman Catholic and Presbyterian churches and, to a lesser extent, the Anglican and Methodist churches have been promoting vocational schools of their own or supporting others. They have also given out direct relief aid to various communities. Under welfare programs, both local and international NGOs have supported select groups, households, institutions, and communities with food assistance and educational, health, and sanitation projects. Disadvantaged women, malnourished children, and street children are receiving special attention in many of the NGO projects.

Although the NGOs are important players in the mix of institutions concerned with social and economic development in Ghana, the nature and organization of their activities also raise some problems and challenges. For example, although NGOs relieve the government of some pressure in the provision of safety nets in urban areas, questions remain about the sustainability of their interventions. In Ghana, these agencies tend to favour capacity-building over the provision of direct relief. Ultimately, this may be seen as constructive, but a certain level of direct-relief assistance remains critical in emergencies and in cases of chronic dependency.

A second issue emerges in the context of democratization in Ghana and relates to potential incompatibilities between processes of social-policy design and delivery and notions of accountability. In this respect, important questions are increasingly being raised about the role of NGOs in social development in relation to that of the state.

Ghana's former Finance Minister, Dr Kwesi Botchwey, suggested in a speech at the Maastricht Meeting of the Global Coalition for Africa (November 1995) that NGOs were usurping the role of the state (Botchwey 1995). This statement was made in response to growing international support for the use of NGOs to ensure greater transparency in the development initiatives of African countries. With the ERP, the state is perceived to be reassigning its traditional roles and responsibilities to groups that cannot be held accountable in the same manner that an elected government would be. Although concern with this trend is presently evident in only limited circles — often academic ones — it may attain wider and more profound significance as civil society develops and makes demands for greater transparency and accountability.

A last set of difficulties in this area comprises issues in the coordination and coherence of NGO activities within the broader network of institutions involved in development. Because of the recent significant increase in the number and types of NGOs operating in Ghana, it has become apparent that their activities in many districts have been uncoordinated with those of other agencies with similar goals. Historically, the location of NGO-supported welfare projects has been largely determined by requests from local communities. Consequently, the spread of facilities and services within and across districts has been uneven.

Donors and social policy

Donors have also contributed significantly to social-development efforts in Ghana. Most directly, of course, donors have engaged in a sort of de facto social policy through their own activities and specific projects. For example, the European Union agreed to assist Ghana in the areas of health, education, private-sector development, governance, human rights, and poverty alleviation. The UNDP is assisting Ghana under the 5th Country Program in the priority areas of capacity-building, private-sector development, and poverty reduction. Other bilateral donors, including the Canadian International Development Agency and the Department for International Development in the United Kingdom, are focusing on health, education, private-sector development, and poverty reduction. World Bank and Japanese assistance go further and attach importance to infrastructure development and the energy sector. Whereas a great many similar interventions have been undertaken through NGOs, most have been implemented through weak public-sector agencies.

In addition to giving such direct interventions and support, however, donors have also functioned as catalysts or lobbyists for the coordination of their activities with national plans and institutions. The NAPPR resulted from donor pressure on the government to articulate its own position on poverty reduction and to develop a specific institutional framework for combating poverty. Moreover, for the purpose of supporting reform and coherence in social policy, bilateral donors have also insisted on the creation of a National Steering Committee for poverty reduction which would coordinate both national policies and donor programs. Donors had complained of having difficulty ascertaining government priorities and the areas in which donors could be of maximum use in fighting poverty. This was because most public agencies applied different criteria in their contacts with donor agencies. Donors pushed for the creation of the National Steering Committee, to be headed by a direct representative of the president and assisted by an NDPC technical committee on poverty.

However, the major role donors have come to play in Ghana's social and economic development has raised important questions about sustainability. As we have seen, despite attempts to coordinate donor and government efforts under NAPPR, most actors continue to pay mere lip service to the document and to conduct business as usual. Under NAPPR, there are some signs that a number of NGOs intend to move away from their former practice of citing programs in an ad hoc and arbitrary manner to one that is more strategic, coordinated by district councils. However, because of the general weakness of the program, problems with coordination can be expected to persist.

Further issues concern local control of social policies and programs and an emerging relative imbalance between donors and Ghana's government in commitment to social policy and influence over it. Generally speaking, local ownership is considered important to the sustainability of social-development projects. However, a recent study of aid effectiveness (Aryeetey 1995) observed that a very significant number of project proposals are submitted to the Ministry of Finance long after the donor and the recipient institution have made contact. The study concluded that about 35% of proposals for bilateral projects were prepared with significant donor input, but project design was either completely or partially controlled by the donor. The Ministry of Finance often sees no justification for direct donor involvement in the preparation of proposals and preliminary designs. Both donors and recipients agree that quite a number of projects have been the outcome of informal suggestions from consultants, picked up by various departments and ministries but unrepresentative of institutional priorities (Aryeetey 1996). On a number of occasions, donors have believed that ministries and departments were too slow in submitting proposals and have tried to jump-start the process. In a number of cases, this procedure has been accepted by recipient institutions, in recognition of their own deficiencies.

Finally, as suggested above, there are indications that foreign aid to various sectors in Ghana has begun to substitute for some government expenditure, particularly for social-sector spending. Although overseas development assistance (ODA) is relatively small in relation to GDP, aid to a number of key social sectors is becoming increasingly important to the government's commitments in those sectors. Social-sector allocations from ODA grew faster than government social-sector expenditure between 1988 and 1993 (Table 2). ODA has increased in education, health, and humanitarian aid and relief. This part of ODA averaged 18% of government spending on social services in this period. The more rapid growth of the ratio of social-sector ODA to government social-sector expenditure came about as a result of slow growth and a proportionate decline in government spending in the social sector, as we explained earlier. We have already suggested key factors accounting for reductions in government spending.

In summary, this trend in social-sector aid does not suggest a stable commitment to social policy from Ghana's government; rather, it suggests that the government seeks to pass the responsibility for social development on to other groups, including external actors, if possible. This implies a smaller role for government, consistent with the neoliberal ideology of the economic-reform strategy as a whole. The implications of this trend are potentially serious. Most obviously, if ODA decreases, which seems highly likely, as a result of increasing donor fatigue, then the burden will shift back to the government. The government will have to either cut the social sectors or reallocate its budget.

Conclusion: issues and directions for Ghanaian social policy

This chapter argues that over the last three decades, Ghana has followed a disparate set of policies to attain some not always properly or explicitly defined social goals. A lack of government commitment to social development has been reflected in the poor articulation of a coherent and credible national social policy and increasingly limited public allocations of resources in this sphere. Across a range of sectors, policies, and programs, the system has consistently failed to direct resources to the people most in need and to ensure that these people have access to services. Lack of political will, implementation difficulties, limited institutional capacities, and competing economic objectives and priorities have all worked to undermine efforts to give more concerted attention to social policy and social development. Reforms in the social sectors under the ERP have tended to reinforce poverty and inequality, rather than effectively addressing them. In the wake of current reforms, the challenges for social development in Ghana are significant and raise a range of issues and questions deserving research and policy consideration. We review some of these issues and questions.

Sustainability

Sustainability is the issue with the broadest scope for the government of Ghana. Given that foreign ODA is replacing a significant amount of government spending, the government must come to grips with the long-term implications of this as aid diminishes. Moreover, cost-recovery mechanisms provide no easy answers, particularly from a social-development perspective. As Norton et al. (1995, p. 48) noted,

> while the amounts charged at the MCH consultations (for immunizations, weighing, and other basic services) may appear small, of the order of 200 cedis [then 0.20 USD] per monthly consultation, the evidence from this study shows that rural women sometimes have difficulty meeting this cost. The poorest mothers are, thus, sometimes compelled to skip immunizations.

Decreasing budgets and ineffective deployment of resources suggest the importance of addressing the national government's ability to develop more sustainable approaches to social-service delivery, particularly by improving its commitments and the methods it uses to identify and reach the most vulnerable groups. Research will have to focus on appropriate mechanisms for social-service delivery that do not burden the government unduly and do not cause greater impoverishment.

Targeting

Providing social services efficiently and sustainably will require increased attention to targeting. As shown in the discussion of PAMSCAD, as well as in the health and education sectors, the government's capacity to target social services is minimal. The government lacks the means to identify recipients on any other than coarse geographical criteria. This allows substantial leakage to occur to unintended beneficiaries. In cases where the government has sought to provide targeting on a narrower basis (such as through exemptions from health user fees), the recipients' poor information and the government's poor monitoring have led to policy failure. One challenge for future research will be to develop low-cost, effective ways to identify recipients.

Decentralization and capacity-building

Targeting requires institutional capacity, particularly in poor areas. Decentralized management of social programs is expected to lead to a more efficient delivery of services to target groups. Local institutions are also clearly inadequately prepared: they lack the funds, the human capacity, and the ability to mobilize the necessary resources. Consider the following quote from the district medical officer at Abura Dunkwa, when asked about how well exemptions for the poor were working: "The exemptions are cumbersome; how do I determine who is a pauper? Besides, my office is not reimbursed for drugs handed out without charge to paupers ... so we cannot be generous in applying the concessions" (Norton et al. 1995, p. 43). Such evidence suggests that the government needs to focus attention and research on rational-decentralization planning and, in particular, fiscal-decentralization measures to help local-government bodies overcome current constraints, in addition to helping them with human and institutional resource- and capacity-building.

Monitoring and evaluation

To build institutional capacity, the government has to do more than just implement its programs at the district level. It also needs to increase its own ability to identify the recipients of social services and monitor the performance of social policies over time. The last national living-standards survey was 6 years ago, and in this time of dynamic change and dramatic decreases in spending, it has become woefully out of date. There may be some promise in this area, as the government is implementing, through the GSS, a Core Welfare Indicators Questionnaire (CWIQ). CWIQ uses basic indicators of poverty to provide quick and ongoing data about different populations. Although this participatory exercise is in some ways a modification of the usual approach to monitoring the standard of living of populations, it may ultimately provide decision-makers with critical, policy-relevant information.

The role of the state

What role should the state play in the delivery of social services? There is no denying the fact that in a developing country like Ghana, the state will inevitably have to be the largest provider of social services. Recognizing, however, that its resources will be inadequate to the task, we note the obvious need to complement this with resources from the private sector, NGOs, and other arms of civil society. If proper complementarity is to be achieved, the state should not reduce budgetary allocations in light of growing contributions from other sources. In addition to maintaining its commitment to social services, the government has to consider appropriate incentives for the private sector to expand its role in a number of areas. For example, the government has to consider fiscal incentives to encourage private doctors to locate in rural areas and support existing health facilities. This would require some research. The government should also consider ways to encourage NGOs to take on the aspects of social-service delivery that are traditionally difficult for state agencies to handle, such as rural water programs. This would require research on the best ways to remunerate NGOs, without burdening the consumer unduly. Partnerships are needed that capitalize on relative advantages without undermining essential state commitments.

Chapter 3

Chile

Progress, Problems, and Prospects

Dagmar Raczynski[1]

Social-policy reforms have been at the forefront of public attention in Chile since the mid-1970s. The objectives of these reforms have gradually expanded to include the search for an effective strategy to fight poverty, improve the efficiency and quality of services, and enhance equity and political inclusion (democratization). In the mid-1970s and 1980s, Chile was a pioneer in adopting neoliberal policies. This orientation included an emphasis on the subsidiary role of the state in the direct provision of services; the reduction and targeting of public expenditures; privatization and decentralization policies; and the prioritization of demand-driven over supply-driven subsidies. However, in the 1990s, concurrent with changes in the internal political and economic context, the debate is being refocused on the social reforms inherited from the neoliberal period. Policy priorities, content, instruments, and institutional arrangements are all being revisited, and although significant continuities exist with previous reforms, the orientations of social policy in democratic Chile suggest the emergence of a new model of social

---

[1] This paper relies heavily on previous work of the author, in particular Raczynski (1994, 1995a, 1995b, 1997, 1998a).

protection, one that departs from the approach of the military regime, as well as from the model prevalent before 1970.

This chapter describes the main principles, dimensions, and content of social-policy reforms in Chile in the mid-1970s, 1980s, and 1990s, identifies obstacles and opportunities for implementation, and as much as possible evaluates outcomes. It begins with an overview of the social-policy system and social situation in Chile before 1970. This is necessary to understand the priorities and implementation of more recent reforms. This chapter is structured according to historical periods. It first describes social policies around 1970, then the reforms of the 1970s and 1980s, and finally those of the 1990s. It concludes with an overview of lessons learned and issues requiring further reflection and study. Annex A of this paper presents a schematic comparison of approaches to social policies in these three periods.

Social protection in Chile to 1970[2]

From 1920 to 1973, Chile's system of social policies entailed increasing state involvement in the direct provision of social services. After the 1929 depression, Chile adopted an import-substitution policy, shut its economy to international trade, and promoted policies to foster the development of national industry and domestic demand. The beginning and later expansion of Chile's public social policies was associated with building the nation-state, a process associated with industrialization, the growth of cities, and weakening of the traditional social order. Upheavals in the urban centres and the mining sector played an important part in the initial push toward state involvement in social issues; so too did emerging social-security laws in European countries, the social Encyclicals of the Roman Catholic Church, and recommendations of international organizations such as the International Labour Organization.

The evolution of the state's approach to social policy during this period was also significantly influenced by the system of political representation and the existing power structure. Through their organizations and political parties, the urban middle sectors, the industrial bourgeoisie, and urban workers pressured the state for policies

---

[2] Unless otherwise stated, the evidence for this section comes from Arellano (1985) and Raczynski (1994).

favourable to them. The result was an increased presence of the state in the economy and society, with political parties playing a central intermediary role. Of note during this period, the organizations of social representation within civil society were weak (Oxhorn 1995), and the gradual extension of the state into economic and social realms tended to limit the role of private entities, the community, and business and labour associations.[3]

This dynamic of state expansion displaced the idea that the state ought to protect only the weakest sectors. Yet, the Chilean welfare state developed in a piecemeal fashion, as a consequence of pressure from various labour and social groups. The final result was a fragmented and inequitable system. By 1970, the entire population was nominally entitled to similar social benefits, but the quality of, and access to, these varied across rural and urban areas, public and private sectors, and different labour categories within each. The most extreme illustration of such fragmentation was Chile's social-security system, which was structured around 35 withholding funds. These funds in turn administered 150 different programs (Foxley et al. 1979).

By the mid-1960s, state activity in the social sectors was significant. At this time, the government prioritized structural reforms affecting property, undertook progressive income and labour policies, and intended to incorporate the urban and rural poor through programs to foster neighbourhood organization (*promoción popular*) in urban areas and agrarian reform and unionization of peasants in rural areas. Further, the government introduced measures to improve salaries and lower the price of basic goods and services. It broadened housing programs and implemented reforms to expand educational coverage at the primary, secondary, and university levels. In 1970, the Popular Unity government accelerated structural reforms that directly affected wealth. Agricultural expropriations were massive, and the government created an area of collective property in industry under state control. Policies in education and health were oriented to creating unified national services (Servicio Unico de Salud [unified health service] and Enseñanza Nacional Unificada [unified national education]). These policies generated strong political opposition and failed.

---

[3] These characteristics are not exclusive to Chile. On the expansion of the social-security system, see Mesa-Lago (1978). For a more general discussion on the role of the state, political parties, and private entities, see among others Garretón (1994) and Kliksberg (1994).

Throughout these years, public social spending expanded significantly. In 1970, such spending was 70% higher than that in 1965, representing 20% of the gross domestic product (GDP); by 1972, it had reached 26% of GDP. It is significant, however, that this expansion was not adequately financed, and this contributed to fiscal deficits and accelerated inflationary tendencies that annulled initial improvements in the monetary incomes of the population. By 1973, the public deficit had become unmanageable, reaching 30% of GDP. Economic problems, major political mobilizations by the opposition, and sharp political conflicts unseated the government. The crisis of 1972-73 was not impetuous but the culmination of unresolved economic and political conflicts that had been mounting for decades (Bitar 1979; Foxley 1983).

The military coup of September 1973 brought an end to five decades of continuous expansion of publicly financed and often state-administered social services. By 1973, Chile's social-policy system had experienced numerous successes but had also accumulated important difficulties. On the positive side, Chile had an infrastructure and supply of social services that benefited increasingly larger portions of the population: first the workers, then the urban middle- and lower-income strata, and finally, then, to a lesser extent, the rural population. By 1970, 94% of the population aged 6-14 years had access to elementary education, and 90% of students were enrolled in the free-of-charge public school system. Thirty-eight percent of adolescents aged 15-18 years were enrolled in high school; and 8% of the population aged 19-24 years were at university. About 90% of live births received immediate medical attention, and almost 90% of children under 6 years of age were covered by national child check-up, nutrition, and immunization programs. The Servicio Nacional de Salud (SNS, national health service), established in 1952, provided the bulk of this wide coverage, owning and managing around 90% of the health-care facilities in Chile. About 70% of the labour force was covered by the social-security system. The state was also directly involved in 60% of the housing units built each year.

Concurrent with processes of economic growth and industrialization, social policies contributed to improvements in human-development indicators. General- and child-mortality rates, which in 1920 were at 30 and 259 per 1 000, respectively, dropped to 9 and 73 per 1 000 by 1972. Illiteracy for people aged 15 years and over fell from 37% in 1920 to 11% in 1970. The proportion of the urban population with access to potable water and sewage increased in 1972 from nil to 65% and 35%, respectively. Life expectancy at birth rose by more than 10 years from 1952 to 1970. The birth rate was more than 40 per 1 000 in 1930, and by 1972 it had dropped to 27 per 1 000. Fertility rates for the same periods dropped from 5.5 children to 3.6 children for women who had completed their fertile years. Also, the social structure in Chile was becoming increasingly urban centred. The urban population was 52% in 1940 and 75% in 1970, with increasing concentration in the metropolitan area of Santiago. Middle and lower strata in the cities benefited the most, particularly from job opportunities created in the public sector, which had expanded and, by 1970, absorbed 12% of the labour force (Muñoz et al. 1980). Overall, public social programs in Chile during this period achieved high coverage, compared with other Latin American countries.

Despite these accomplishments, ample room remained in all social programs to make the distribution of benefits more equitable. Also, the system was costly and plagued by administrative inefficiencies. It was highly centralized, with vertical bureaucratic decision-making processes; suffered rigidity and an incapacity to respond to the basic needs of the population; had geographic and economic inequalities; and paid low wages to professionals and functionaries. Social-policy decision-making was based on scattered information. For example, basic data on the size, characteristics, and geographical distribution of poverty and evidence of the beneficiaries of public spending were almost nonexistent. Later, studies revealed that income-based poverty affected 17% of households; and poverty was not uniform, in that people who were poor in one respect (for example, housing) were not necessarily so in another (for example, children's education or household income) (ODEPLAN and Universidad Católica de Chile 1975; Cortázar 1977). The first rigorous study on beneficiaries of public spending was published in 1979 (Foxley et al. 1979).

Further, the country had unsatisfied needs for health care, a growing housing deficit, population sectors marginalized from social security, and high repetition and drop out rates in education, particularly in rural areas and in urban areas with high concentrations of poverty. Although the majority of the population was formally covered, access to services was often limited. In the 1960s, the criticisms of the public social system grew particularly acute, concurrent with stagnation in economic growth, inflationary trends, the exacerbation of political conflicts, and social mobilizations around measures affecting the rights and the distribution of property.

Social-policy reforms in the mid-1970s and 1980s

The economic and political context

In the early 1970s, Chile experienced severe economic imbalances and sociopolitical conflict. The military government, which took power in September 1973, remained in place for 17 years, until March 1990. The ideology and doctrine of the government crystallized around a model that was both economically neoliberal and politically authoritarian, breaking sharply with the development strategy that had prevailed from 1930. Changes occurred in a closed political system that was characterized by strict control over social organizations (particularly political parties, unions, and professional associations), collective expressions of social demands, and the media.

With the advent of the military regime, an open economy replaced a closed and protected one. A strategy that favoured external demand and the growth of exports succeeded one that favoured import substitution, with the twin pillars of strengthening the industrial sector and internal demand. The state, which had strongly supported economic development, came to play a less interventionist role, limiting itself to the formulation of macroeconomic policies. Economic policies involved the privatization of commercial firms and banks, liberalization of prices (except wages), reduction of import tariffs, the free movement of capital, and a strict fiscal regime. The main elements of revised labour policies were promotion of labour flexibility, limitations on the power of labour unions and collective bargaining, and the reduction of labour costs. Economic adjustment and macroeconomic equilibria came to take precedence over social-policy concerns.

With this neoliberal reorientation, Chile saw more than a decade of economic instability. In 1975/76 and again in 1982/83, Chile experienced a major drop in GDP, and in 1988 and 1989, after precrisis levels were regained, it had the highest growth in Latin

America. The net result was a moderate annual growth rate of 2.6%, inferior to the rate between 1961 and 1971, which had reached 4.6%. After 1986, however, the economy began a sustained recovery and expansion, which coincided with an increase in state regulation, particularly in the financial sector, and a macroeconomic policy focused on domestic and foreign balance. The country experienced growth, investment, and the creation of jobs. Unemployment, which had averaged 13.7% between 1974 and 1988, dropped to around 9% in 1989, and real wages rose modestly. Together, these trends resulted in declining levels of income-based poverty from 1985 on. Whereas in 1990, 34% of households had an income below the poverty line (11% below the extreme poverty, or indigent, line), in 1985 and 1987 the figures were 45 and 38%, respectively (25 and 13% being below the indigent line) (Torche 1987; MIDEPLAN n.d. for 1987, 1990).

Despite these achievements, in 1990 poverty figures were still double those prevailing 20 years earlier. Moreover, the neoliberal economic strategy pursued under the military regime exacerbated distributive inequalities. In Greater Santiago, the share in total income of the poorest 40% of families, which fluctuated between 12 and 13% in 1965-73, fell to 11% in 1974-81 and to less than 10% in 1982-85. The Gini coefficient increased from 0.50 in 1970 to 0.55 in 1984 (Riveros 1984). In addition, surveys of household spending in 1969, 1978, and 1988 revealed a decline in household expenditures for the three lowest quintiles, the decline being greater in the poorest households. By contrast, the richest quintile alone increased its level of expenditure from 44.5% in 1969 to 54.6% in 1988 (Raczynski 1994, table 15).

A neoliberal approach to social policies

Oriented by the neoliberal model, Chile's military government pursued three general objectives in restructuring the country's social policies: first, it redefined the purpose, objectives, and spaces for public action in the social sectors; second, it modified institutional arrangements within the social sectors; and third, it reduced social expenditures and modified priorities and mechanisms for financing and allocating resources.

In contrast to the previous period, the objectives of social policy after 1973 were subordinated to the goals of controlling inflation.

Economic growth took precedence over redistributive and social objectives, the latter being limited to the alleviation of extreme poverty. Neoliberal policies aimed at restricting the role of the state, which in practice entailed reducing public spending and transferring the administration of social services to entities closer to the population, such as municipalities and the private sector. The dominant philosophy was that state-financed social programs should benefit only those households not in a position to meet their own most urgent basic needs; that the allocation of public resources to address social problems should be governed by demand- rather than supply-side forces; that subsidies should be transferred directly to beneficiaries; and that financing for social services should be based on services effectively rendered and not on static or historically based allocation schedules. Policies guided by these principles, it was asserted, would ensure that resources reached the poorest sectors effectively and encourage market competition, thus promoting efficiency in the management and delivery of social services. Castañeda (1992) described the principles and objectives of the reforms.

The most significant of these reforms were implemented in the 1980s. The 1970s had been a period of normalization, rationalization, and preparation for the reform projects. This decade was marked by significant reductions in public spending; the implementation of measures to eliminate some obvious inequities in social security and in health; targeting of the state's activities, particularly in education and health; development of a social safety net; completion of diagnostic studies on the magnitude, location, and characteristics of poverty; and development of poverty-screening instruments. During this time, the government also introduced the so-called modernizing reforms: the Administrative and Regionalization Reform, the Social Security Reform, and the Presidential Directive on Education and the Restructuring of Health. The main reforms and measures that affected the social sectors are summarized below (see also Table 1).

Fiscal balance and public expenditures

For the military government, a commitment to fiscal balance governed public spending. In the 1970s, the government had pursued this balance by implementing a tax reform, which simplified the existing system and launched a successful campaign against evasion and by reducing expenditures. At the end of the 1980s, when the economy

Table 1. Chilean social-policy reforms: 1973–90.

Axis of reform	Social sector	Reforms and policies implemented
Public social expenditures		Reducing expenditures from 20–25% in 1970 to 15% in 1989
Targeting	Education	Transferring expenditures from the university to preschool and elementary education Targeting of specific programs within the educational system (e.g., school food programs) Revoking state-subsidized free university education
	Health	Concentrating expenditures on the primary level and on children's (i.e., under age 6 years) health and nutrition programs Revoking free curative care in public establishments (except for children and pregnant women) Introducing copayment rules, according to level of income
	Social safety net	Designing a social safety net Designing national instruments to screen the poor population and to identify actual beneficiaries of social programs
Decentralization		Defining a new regional administrative division across the country Decentralizing government, partially, from the ministries to the regions Creating FNDR Redefining, legally, the functions and roles of the municipalities
	Health	Disaggregating SNS into 26 health services
	Education and social safety net	Transferring administration to the municipalities
Privatization	Social security	Creating an individual capitalization system, administered by the private sector
	Health	Creating private for-profit health-insurance institutions
	Education	Creating incentives for the private administration of state-financed schools and for the creation of private post-secondary (i.e., university, technical centres) training institutions
	Education, health, housing	Outsourcing of specific services to the private sector
Demand- or supply-driven subsidies	Health, education	Allocating resources according to services rendered (e.g., school enrollment, health services delivered)
	Housing	Introducing demand subsidy (i.e., voucher)

Source: Raczynski (1995a).
Note: FNDR, Fondo Nacional de Desarrollo Regionala (national regional development fund); SNS, Servicio Nacional de Salud (national health service).

was growing, the government lowered taxes on the basis of two assumptions: that economic growth would generate enough funds to finance public spending and that a reduction in tax rates would stimulate savings and investments and thereby accelerate economic growth.

In accordance with these decisions, per capita public spending dropped sharply in 1973-76, relative to the level prevalent in 1970. It recovered toward the late 1970s, parallel to the economic upswing of these years, and then dropped again during the economic crisis of 1982 and did not recover. Cutbacks occurred — particularly in housing, education, and health — and these affected investments and wages more than operational costs (Marshall 1981; Cabezas 1988; MHDP 1997).

Targeting and poverty alleviation

The government's targeting policy had numerous components. In education and health, spending was restructured intrasectorally (that is, priority was given to the less complex levels of care). Public investments in education and health, which dropped significantly, targeted primarily isolated and socially underprivileged areas. Emergency employment programs, welfare pensions, child subsidies, nursery schools, and community child-care facilities for poor families were created to assist the extremely poor segments of the population (Vergara 1990; Raczynski and Romaguera 1995). Nevertheless, despite targeting efforts, the percentage of fiscal spending that effectively reached the poorest sectors was low. In 1987, social expenditures constituted 13% of GDP; the goods and services that were directly distributed to people, 7% of GDP; and the social spending that directly benefited the poorest 20% of households, 2.2% of GDP. If the poorest 40% of households are considered, the latter figure reached 3.6% of GDP (Haindl et al. 1989). Still, the safety net played an important role in the survival strategies adopted by the poorest households (Raczynski and Serrano 1985; Raczynski 1987).

The literature on the Chilean experience with targeting points to a number of lessons that are worth noting (Vergara 1990; Raczynski 1992, 1995b; Sojo 1990; Grosh 1992; de Kadt 1993). Among the most important of these are the following:

- The preexistence of universal programs facilitates the introduction of targeting, as demonstrated by the experience with the implementation of successful health-nutrition programs for mothers and children at risk (Raczynski and Oyarzo 1981; Raczynski 1987; Vergara 1990).

- In a situation of diminished public resources and heightened social needs, strict targeting may transform programs that traditionally invested in human capital through purely welfare-oriented assistance programs and discouraged the initiatives and efforts of family members to generate income by their own effort.

- Reliable information is a critical precondition for targeting. The information required is not limited to that obtained through screening the poor population. Targeting also requires assessments of the specific situations a program seeks to modify, the most efficient means to achieve the goal, the size of the target group, and identification of expeditious ways of reaching this group.

- There is no single mechanism to facilitate targeting, and a socioeconomic screening instrument that focuses on households is not necessarily the best. This type of instrument has considerable administrative costs, is vulnerable to unreliable information and discretionary decisions on the part of those who apply it, and often implies social stigmatization. Targeting can be implemented through program design or with reference to territorial areas, household-screening instruments, or information on risk and vulnerable groups obtained from regular services registers. Notably, preference for one or another targeting mechanism is not independent of perceptions of poverty and its determinants. If poverty is seen as rooted in individual causes (for example, characteristics of the poor person or family), a poor–nonpoor screening instrument will be privileged, the assumption being that direct transfers to the poor will take him or her out of poverty. Alternatively, if poverty is perceived to be rooted in more systemic or environmental causes, the priority will be to modify these dimensions, and targeting by geographical areas or by type of service offered will be seen as more appropriate. (For a more complete discussion of targeting mechanisms see Grosh [1992] and Raczynski [1995b].) The suitability of one or the other, or a combination of these approaches, depends on the objectives and nature of the social program, the magnitude and characteristics of poverty, institutional factors, and the availability and cost of timely and reliable information.

- It is an error to assume that targeting will increase the effectiveness of social expenditures. A very well targeted program may have no effect whatsoever on the living conditions of its beneficiaries. The impact of a program on poverty depends more on its specific objectives, content, and coverage (that is, error of exclusion) of poor groups than on its spillover to nonpoor groups.

Probably the most beneficial impact of Chile's targeting policy in the 1970s and 1980s was the diffusion of the idea itself, along with improvements in the technical management of social programs. Included among such improvements were the development of baseline studies; economic assessments of programs; identification of the actual beneficiaries of social spending; implementation of standardized educational testing to determine achievement of minimum learning objectives; and regular measurement of the nutritional status of children of less than 6 years of age in public (municipal) health facilities.

Decentralization policies

Chile's military government implemented a political-administrative reform with two axes: regionalization and municipalization. With respect to regionalization, three territorial levels — regional, provincial, and municipal — were created below the national level, decentralizing the functions and tasks of the state ministries and creating Fondo Nacional de Desarrollo Regionala (FNDR, national regional development fund) to transfer resources for small investments to regional authorities. Also, the SNS, the central agency of the Chilean health sector, was subdivided into 26 territorial units.

Although decentralization aimed at relegating some activities to subnational levels, in fact no significant decision-making power or resource was transferred to the regional levels. The resources administered by the FNDR were never more than 8% of public investment. Moreover, regional, provincial, and municipal authorities were all appointed by the presidency, and the participation of regional and local actors, organizations, and agents was either nonexistent or under strict control (Raczynski and Serrano 1985; Serrano 1996). The subdivision of the SNS into 26 smaller geographical services did not effectively decentralize this area of social policy, as the means to finance and to define priorities, programs, and procedures were all retained by the national ministry (Celedón and Oyarzo 1998).

The government created a new municipal regime and transferred various functions, responsibilities, and resources to the municipalities. Municipalities were to analyze social problems, administer the social safety net, manage educational and health establishments, and formulate specific social projects to address problems specific to their area. Beginning in the 1980s, the central government provided incentives to transfer public education and primary health care to the municipalities. Initially, the process was voluntary in that municipalities requested the transfer, and they received economic compensation, administrative support, and technical assistance. These transfers were frozen during the economic crisis of 1982–83 and were reinitiated in 1986. Transfers were then massively imposed on the municipalities, without any special economic rewards, technical assistance, preparation, or training (Raczynski and Serrano 1987, 1988; Espínola 1991; Raczynski and Romaguera 1995; Serrano 1995). By 1989, municipalities managed almost 100% of the public educational establishments and urban and rural health clinics and posts. The transfer included real estate, equipment, and all personnel. Notably, the latter ceased to be state employees, losing both labour rights and benefits associated with their previous positions. This promoted significant opposition to the transfer.

Again, however, as with regionalization, there were difficulties. The municipalities restructured according to a centrally designed formula, which left little flexibility for local adaptation. Moreover, although municipalities received more resources than in the past, they had little managerial autonomy, as a large proportion of the resources was tied to specific activities. Also, after the economic crisis of 1982–83, the resources transferred to municipalities were not adjusted to account for inflation. The result was the development of significant municipal deficits incurred to meet the costs of administering educational and health establishments (Espínola 1991; Miranda 1990).

Initially, the government had hoped that municipalities would contribute their own resources, thereby increasing local-level social expenditures. To some extent this did occur. In 1990, the municipal share was a full 12% of education and health expenditures (Stewart and Ranis 1992, table 5). Yet, this only partially compensated for the decrease in central-government spending. Additionally, and not unexpectedly, only a few municipalities had enough per capita revenue to support education, health, and poverty programs. (Chile's municipalities possess no independent revenue-raising power.) Most municipalities were at the other extreme: low per capita revenue and high concentration of poverty. A fund legislated to redistribute resources from rich to poor municipalities — the Fondo Común Municipal (common municipal fund) — was oriented in the right direction, but the size of this fund was insufficient to overcome the enormous initial territorial inequities (Raczynski and Cabezas 1988).

Finally, studies of municipal performance in the 1980s showed that local administrations were overwhelmed by requirements and poorly coordinated instructions from the central government. They were also saddled with responsibility for the direct provision of welfare benefits and for extensive administrative tasks. Lacking the necessary conceptual and practical tools to engage in effective or efficient social development, municipalities acted independently only exceptionally. Autonomous social projects tended to be scarce, discontinuous, and palliative, rather than preventive (Raczynski and Serrano 1998).

In sum, the decentralization policy of the military government made significant changes in social policies but ran up against a range of difficulties. Despite these challenges, the policy helped to legitimize the idea of decentralization and define a conceptual and practical basis for local social development in Chile. For example, in 1989–90, only the professional associations of teachers and medical and paramedical personnel demanded recentralizing measures to give them back their lost labour rights, particularly the rights against dismissal and to have wages scale up with seniority.

Privatization-oriented reforms

Before the 1970s, the provision of social services in Chile was primarily in the hands of the state. After 1973, however, the military government introduced the partial or full privatization of some services.

The private administration of publicly subsidized services — Outsourcing and the private administration of publicly subsidized services were stimulated, although this strategy had variable results.

Outsourcing was applied to nonmedical services in public hospitals and to food preparation within the national school food program. The experience was positive, with delivery of better quality goods or services at lower cost, so long as unambiguous definitions were provided of the goods or services to be outsourced and of the standards to be monitored.

By contrast, the private administration of publicly financed social services had mixed results. The administration of vocational high schools by business associations met with success, with improvements in the quality and relevance of the training for the productive sector, as well as enhanced funding from the business sector for the schools. Enrollment in state-subsidized, privately administered schools went up from 14% in 1980 to 30% in 1985. This expansion was associated with the introduction of a monthly student subsidy, Unidad de Subsidio Escolar (USE, unit for school subsidy). The expansion of these schools stopped in the mid-1980s with the failure to readjust the subsidy for inflation. Yet, a debate persists in the country regarding this experience. A national test, Prueba SIMCE (Sistema de Medición de la Calidad de la Educación [system for measurement of quality of education]), which measures the achievement of educational objectives, showed slightly higher scores and probably higher variability in scores in schools under private administration than in municipal schools. For some, this result suggests better quality of education and more efficient use of resources. For others, this interpretation is spurious, as the privately administered, state-subsidized schools enrol children from more advantaged socioeconomic backgrounds or represent schools managed by private, nonprofit foundations (including religious congregations) supported with resources additional to those of the state.

The private administration of public hospitals was a pilot experiment that failed, faltering on lack of decentralization of the health services; cumbersome legislation and administrative procedures; and a clash between the organizational culture and decision-making logic of the physicians — traditional hospital administrators in Chile — and those of the economists, engineers, and administrators.

In the housing sector, the selection of sites and the construction of housing units were also subcontracted to the private sector. Although the state defined the size of units, it possessed no adequate means to control the quality of construction and provided no norms regarding neighbourhood equipment and availability of basic services. The result was that new residential areas for the poor and lower middle strata appeared on the outskirts of cities where the price of land was cheaper, exacerbating geographical segregation within the large cities.

In sum, a review of the Chilean experience suggests that the impact of private administration depends on a number of factors, including the traits of private administrators, economic incentives, legislation, administrative procedures, the strength of the organizational culture prevalent in the services that are privatized, and monitoring and evaluation processes that the state is able to develop and apply.

Privatization of social services — Beginning in the 1980s, the government undertook the full privatization of some key social services. The most important were in social security and in health. Other privatization reforms took place in post-secondary education (that is, universities and other higher education training centres) and in labour training. The pay-as-you-go social-security system was replaced with an individual capitalization system managed by the private sector and regulated by the state. Under the new system, contributions (10% of gross wages) are accumulated in individual accounts for workers. Pensions are drawn from funds accumulated over 20 or more years, managed by private corporations, Administradoras de Fondos de Pensiones (AFPs, administrators of pension funds), that invest the funds in the financial market, under state regulation. The new system is mandatory, as was the old, and workers are free to choose at all times the AFP they wish to join. The state guarantees a minimum return, based on the average return of the system in a given period, and a minimum pension for workers who, having accumulated funds for 20 or more years, lack enough savings to finance a pension above the legally established minimum. It also guarantees a welfare pension for poor people more than 65 years of age who contributed for less than 20 years (or not at all) to social security (Arellano 1985; Marcel and Arenas 1991).

There was a rapid and massive transfer of wage earners to the new system, encouraged by economic incentives (for example, increase in net wages through a reduction in the mandatory social-security contributions in the new system), declining benefits in the old system during the years immediately prior to the reform, and a general lack of trust in the old system. The new system has come to play a central role in the expansion and functioning of Chile's financial market.

Conclusions about the success of the social-security reforms can only be tentative. In the protection of income levels of the population during periods of sickness and old age, the new system eliminates the demographic impasse that pay-as-you-go systems face as the population ages. Yet, its final test for Chile is pending — until it pays a majority of the pensions. So far, the social-security system has been accumulating funds — in 1994, these constituted more than 43% of gross national product — and has been paying out no more than 15% of the total number of monthly civilian pensions. On average, the value of pensions has been higher under the new system. The returns earned by the funds accumulated in each individual account depend on the behaviour of the financial market, and so far the average performance of this market has been favourable, particularly up to the early 1990s. Steady economic growth and stability are fundamental to the system. National and global crises, like the one in 1981, might easily destabilize it.

The coverage of the system can be measured as the percentage of the employed labour force that is affiliated and regularly pays its mandatory contributions, and this has not surpassed the figure prevalent before the reform, fluctuating around 60%. People have a high level of uncertainty concerning the future size of state-guaranteed pensions. Moreover, the system registers high administrative costs, augmented by the high rate of rotation between AFPs resulting from publicity and competition.

Another important privatizing reform of the military government was in the health sector. The creation of private health services was preceded by sharp debates between government authorities and the powerful Asociación Gremial del Colegio Médico (national medical association). Many issues were intertwined in the debate: the role of the public and private sector; the priorities of health-care policy; the amount of resources allocated to health care; the reorganization of the public sector; the salaries, training opportunities, and labour conditions of physicians and other health-care staff; and the participation of the medical association and physicians in the decision-making and management of health care (Raczynski 1983). The initial proposals for privatization gradually evolved to support a mixed, ill-defined public–private system. The social-security reform permitted affiliates to place their mandatory health-care contributions that previously went automatically to the public health-care fund in private health institutions, Instituciones de Salud Previsional (ISAPREs, institutions for provisional health). Affiliates that opt for the private system enter into an annual contract with an ISAPRE that in turn establishes the monthly amount to be paid, the health care that is included, and reference fees and discounts. Health-care plans offered by the ISAPREs vary, depending on age, sex, and family size, as well as varying in terms of benefits, freedom of choice regarding the physician and treatment facility, amount of reimbursement, and exclusions or blackout periods. At present, there are more than 8 000 plans, rendering comparative analysis impossible, particularly as each ISAPRE uses a different unit to define the monthly age–sex costs of a plan, its benefits, and its reimbursement fees. The result is a lack of transparency in the market for health-insurance plans. Affiliation with a specific ISAPRE is highly unstable, and individuals frequently change from one ISAPRE to another and from the ISAPRE system to Fondo Nacional de Salud (national health fund) (Miranda 1990; CIEPLAN–CORSAPS–FLACSO 1996; Celedón and Oyarzo 1998).

The private system expanded slowly up to 1985 but more quickly from then on, as a consequence of government decisions resulting in increased economic incentives for the private sector. These incentives included an increase in health-care contributions from 4% to 6%, then in 1985 to 7%, of earnings; the transfer (in 1986) of financial responsibility for the maternity subsidy from the ISAPREs to the state; and the option for employers to make a 2%, tax-deductible increase in their contribution to the premiums of their workers who earned close to the minimum wage (Miranda 1990; CIEPLAN–CORSAPS–FLACSO 1996). The number of ISAPRE affiliates also increased through economic growth and rising wages. However, the health system that has resulted is effectively dividing the population into two groups: a high-income–low-risk group and a low-income–high-risk group. The private sector (the ISAPREs) cares for the former, and the public sector cares for the latter. The care of each is financed by mandatory health contributions, the absolute amount of which is tied to the level of the worker's wage.

The transfer of the care of higher-income groups to the ISAPREs meant a reduction in health quotas for the public sector. In 1994, the ISAPREs provided curative care for 27% of the population and collected more than 65% of the resources paid in as mandatory health contributions. The public sector collected 35% of the contributions and provided preventive health care for the entire population and curative care for around 60-65% of the population (CIEPLAN-CORSAPS-FLACSO 1996). Low-risk–high-income groups tend to be overinsured in the ISAPRE system. Moreover, when that population ages and lowers its earned income as a result of retirement or any other cause, it must pay considerable additional premiums to the ISAPRE or switch back to the public system. Estimates show that average contributions paid by people more than 60 years of age are 150% higher than the average premiums for young adults. Thus, the public system operates as a reinsurance mechanism for the private system. Under these circumstances, and as a consequence of the population's aging process and changes in the epidemiological profile, increased costs for the state are to be expected in the future. In sum, the links between the public and private sectors are detrimental to the former and are socially regressive. In addition to the disadvantages described above, there are others. Most notably are the drain of qualified professionals from the public to the private sector and the tendency of public-sector beneficiaries to be dissatisfied with services available compared with those provided by the private sector.

It is important to note that the expansion of the ISAPRE system has encouraged for-profit health investments and led to the creation of a significant network of medical infrastructure in urban and high-income areas. This in turn has contributed to an emigration of professional resources from the public to the private sector. Private health investors currently represent a powerful interest group that has divided the unity of Asociación Gremial del Colegio Médico (national medical association) and diminished its traditional commitment to social medicine. In the 1990s, this private-sector interest group has played a central role in creating obstacles to new reforms. Other studies (CIEPLAN–CORSAPS–FLACSO 1996; Celedón and Oyarzo 1998) give a more complete, critical discussion of the interaction between the public and the ISAPRE systems, and the implications of this interaction for vulnerable groups.

Allocation of resources: demand- and supply-driven subsidies

The social reforms introduced by the military government included a greater reliance on market mechanisms to improve efficiency. Specifically, the government encouraged competition for clients and users among public establishments of a similar type (for example, schools, health posts) by means of demand-driven subsidies. To allocate resources to schools and health services, the government put in place mechanisms that tied resources to levels of activity or usage. This approach required setting a price for the services rendered, a difficult task, particularly in the case of health. In education, the schools received a subsidy (the USE), according to the average level of students in attendance the previous month. The value varied according to the level of education but did not reflect variation in costs resulting from urban or rural setting, geographical accessibility, or poverty. After the 1982–83 crisis, the USE was not adjusted for inflation, and in 1989 it was worth 19% less than in 1982. This resource squeeze resulted in a decrease in teachers' wages. Also, as the economic resources of schools were contingent on students in actual attendance, teachers dedicated a significant proportion of their time to tracking down pupils. Overall, attention to student performance lapsed throughout the educational system (Espínola 1991).

In the health sector, resources were allocated through a mechanism that linked a range of different services with specific reimbursement fees. Health establishments received part of their resources (about 25%) according to the number and type of services provided during the previous month. The remaining percentage was allocated according to historical criteria and the number and type of personnel. As in the education sector, the real value of health subsidies deteriorated after the 1982–83 crisis. Also, the reimbursement fee for some activities was lower and for others it was higher than the real cost of the service, creating incentives for overbilling. These incentives also led to inflated reports of services rendered. These dynamics generated an increase in expenditures to the point that, in 1983, the government imposed both a ceiling on the amount of resources an establishment could bill for and a return to preexisting allocation mechanisms (Miranda 1990).

The implementation of social-policy reforms

The implementation of policy reforms confronted numerous obstacles. Some lay outside the scope of the policies themselves; however, others arose from imperfections in the design and implementation process. For example, as noted above, decentralization policies relegated tasks at local levels without providing the necessary support (for example, economic resources, training, professional skills) to effectively manage programs. Furthermore, local authorities were appointed or "semi-appointed," in accordance with preferences of the central government, rather than in response to the interests of social-service clients. Moreover, an essential element in an effective process of decentralization was missing: organized and informed local groups, motivated to participate in regional government and local administration. In practice, the central government defined social policies and programs to the smallest detail, and the role of municipalities remained peripheral.

Another important obstacle to effective reform was the nature of the social agents involved. At issue was the tradition in Chile of having a strong state as financer and provider of social services. The force of this tradition prevented or altered the initial proposals for the privatization of health care and education and hampered the decentralization of the state apparatus. Strong opposition to the reforms came particularly from the medical association and the bureaucracy. It is important to register that the country's pre-1973 "institutional and cultural inheritance" (Richards 1997) was an important factor contributing to the positive trends in Chile's human-development indicators and made possible the successful implementation of highly effective targeted health and nutrition programs (Raczynski and Oyarzo 1981; Monckeberg 1984; Vergara 1990; Raczynski 1995b).

An additional obstacle to effective reform was the slow, weak response of the private sector to the privatization policies. The response was slower and weaker than the government had expected, so it was compelled to put particular incentives in place to encourage the private sector to provide public goods. This was an important factor in the creation of the private health-insurance associations.

As a consequence of these difficulties, in the early 1990s the central government continued to be largely responsible for funding and providing health care and education in Chile. About 65% of the population continued to be cared for through the public health system, a percentage only slightly lower than in 1970. Moreover, 90% of the elementary- and high-school enrollment was subsidized by the state, a proportion similar to that in 1970. Only one-third of this enrollment was in private and two-thirds in municipal public schools. The 26 regional health services of the SNS were highly dependent on the programmatic, financial, and operational decisions of the central ministry. Similarly, housing policy decentralized the building and some financing functions to the private sector, yet decisions on programs, selection of beneficiaries, and other aspects remained centralized.

Social policies in the 1990s: toward a new model

Toward a new model of social protection

The socioeconomic legacy of the military government had two general dimensions. On the positive side, Chile possessed an economy in macroeconomic balance, a price system without major distortions, a private sector that was planning its investments for the medium term, and, after 1986, a process of growth that had low inflation and created new jobs. Less positively, however, Chile's society still registered high levels of poverty; increased concentration of income, consumption, and wealth; deteriorated public health services, high housing deficits, educational services with high coverage but low and unequal quality; and social-sector personnel who had been hurt by the social reforms, particularly by those that had modified institutional arrangements and affected labour conditions.

The new democratic government, which assumed power in March 1990, was made up of a centre-left coalition of political parties, the Concertación de Partidos para la Democracia (coalition of parties for democracy), headed by President Aylwin. In March 1994, a new government assumed power of the same coalition of political parties, maintaining continuity with the political and socioeconomic strategy adopted by the first government of the Concertación. This government set out to make economic growth based on private enterprise and export promotion compatible with macroeconomic equilibrium and improved distributive conditions. The government's program was based on three fundamental premises: first, the success of the Chilean economy — based on the experience of the 1980s — depended on its export orientation and its integration into the international financial system; second, international competitiveness and the growth of the economy should be made compatible with greater domestic equity and a more rapid reduction of poverty than the market alone would permit; and, third, the reconstruction and reinforcement of democracy at the political-institutional and local levels was an urgent priority. The government proposed continuity in economic policy, gradual changes in social policies, and a new style of political decision-making. Pizarro et al. (1995) outlined the principles, key initiatives, and some results of the first government of the Concertación. Cortázar (1994) analyzed the achievements and pending issues in the area of labour relations and policies. Weyland (1997) reviewed similar issues addressed in six books published between 1993 and 1995.

On the political front, the new government had to win the trust of national and foreign private investors, maintain macroeconomic balance, and respond to the social demands of the population. To achieve these objectives, it initiated a strategy of political and social agreement (*concertación*, in the sense of cooperation) between business, unions, and political parties, without precedent in the history of the country. The purpose of the initiative was to achieve a common vision of social, economic, and political development among the actors involved and to promote a system of political and social negotiation that would harmonize diverse social demands with each other and with macroeconomic and external restrictions.

The first step toward the Concertación included the so-called Master Agreement, a tax reform, and an amendment to existing labour laws. Under the Master Agreement, labour, business, and government met each year for 4 years and agreed on issues such as the adjustment of wages in the public sector, the value of the minimum wage, and minimum pension rates. This agreement also facilitated the approval in Congress of labour reforms to enhance equity between workers and employers in, for example, labour contracts, unions, collective bargaining, and the right to strike (Cortázar 1994; Pizarro et al. 1995). When the first democratic government took office in 1990, it inherited a "watertight" budget that had been strictly defined by the military government. Funds allocated in the budget to social spending were 7.8% below the commitment made in the 1989 budget.

For the democratic government, as for its military predecessor, the pursuit of fiscal balance was the main criterion in determining the amount of public spending. Moreover, the government preferred to fund public spending through domestic resources and thus avoid external debt. Therefore, tax reform was a central component of the government's approach to budget management, proposed in the presidential campaign. In June 1990, the tax reform was approved by a large majority in Congress, exemplifying a process of negotiation unprecedented in Chilean political tradition (Schkolnik 1992; Pizarro et al. 1995; Marcel 1997). The reform was approved on the understanding that the new resources would be used for social purposes and that the reform would remain in place only until 1994. However, in

1993, before the presidential election, the government negotiated with Congress a new bill to ensure that most of the taxes would remain, thus securing the financing needed for the public spending of the second government of the Concertación. The heated nature of the debate in Congress made it clear that future extensions of the reform or additional taxes would be nearly impossible. In future, additional social spending would have to be funded by economic growth; by new financing mechanisms, such as tariffs, copayments, and tax-exempt donations for social aims; and by improvements to efficiency within the public sector. Some initiatives are currently being implemented to achieve these ends.

Chile's democratic governments: innovations in social policy[4]

Since 1990 two democratic governments in Chile have not only struggled for more resources for provision of social services but also changed the policy space and priorities inherited from the previous administration, revised the institutional framework, and developed innovative policy instruments. Six particularly noteworthy changes are discussed below.

Articulation between social and economic policies

Currently, social policies are perceived by the government as mutually dependent and complementary both to economic and labour policies and to public investment. The guiding principles of the relationship between economic and social policies in democratic Chile are as follows: first, good economic performance is viewed as essential to the goals of equity and poverty reduction; second, given their contribution to strengthening human capabilities, social policies are viewed as investments that contribute to economic growth (rather than as expenses); third, good economic performance is not enough to overcome poverty and ensure social equity — public investments in basic social services for education, health, and sanitary infrastructure are critical, together with specific, complementary policies to target the poor and more vulnerable sectors.

---

[4] This section follows Raczynski (1995a, b, 1998b).

Sociopolitical integration

Strategies for social development presently prioritize not only poverty alleviation but also social integration and political inclusion. A critical goal is to address exclusionary processes in society that affect the most disadvantaged groups, among them the poor and various other segments of the population (for example, women, youth, various ethnic groups). This involves a commitment to empower and strengthen the assets of not only vulnerable groups but also other agents (for example, public institutions, local administrations, entrepreneurs, universities, commercial actors, nongovernmental organizations [NGOs], professionals) to promote opportunities for the less advantaged.

This strategy has two principal components. First, sectoral policies secure a basic level of citizenship to the whole population in the areas of education, health, housing, and social security. Education, particularly the quality and equity of education, is considered of special importance because of its close link with improvements to productivity and international competitiveness. There is also a recognition that social policies must respond to evolving challenges (for example, vulnerabilities associated with the current epidemiological profile; youth training and employment; support to small urban and rural productive units; mental health and drugs).

The second component relates to the nature of policies targeted to the more vulnerable segments of the population. The approach departs centrally from the one inherited from the military government by emphasizing strategies to empower vulnerable groups, rather than distributing assistance or palliatives (that is, direct subsidies to the poor). Community involvement and social participation are favoured, as is support to groups, organizations, and communities, rather than to isolated individuals or families. Programs are intended to support productive capabilities and assets for the poor and other vulnerable sectors. Although measures aimed at poverty alleviation (that is, safety nets) exist for extreme situations, they are not the principal aspect of social policy.

The empowerment approach has translated in time into a demand for a territorial or community-based approach to poverty (Raczynski 1998b). The underlying assumptions are that for vulnerable groups, the place where one lives or works determines one's social opportunities and history of poverty; that the majority of the poor live in communities with high concentrations of poor people; that to fight poverty, it is important to incorporate the characteristics of the places where the poor live or work within the broader societal context; and that in defining specific projects, it is necessary to build simultaneously on the needs, capabilities, and assets of the population, as well as on the development potential of the areas where they live or work. The understanding is that specific projects have to be formulated with the participants and respond to the diversity of poverty situations in economic, organizational, family, and cultural terms.

Targeting

As already noted, targeting is based on the principle that social policies must be selective. Although selectivity is considered a central tenet of policy design in Chile today, it is also recognized that not all social programs need to target the poor; rather, the specifics of targeting have to be decided with reference to concrete programs and contexts. For example, it is generally perceived as inappropriate to target services considered rights acquired by virtue of mandatory contributions (for example, social-security benefits). It is also viewed as inappropriate to target the operating costs of free or subsidized basic education and health services, as these programs are considered fundamental to a minimum level of opportunity for the entire population (Crispi and Marcel 1993). To enhance equity, universal programs must be supplemented by specific programs targeting the most vulnerable groups or the most neglected geographical areas or services. Multiple targeting mechanisms are recognized (for example, socioeconomic screening instruments or targeting by program design, territorial or geographical area, or selection of services), each with its advantages and disadvantages. The suitability of one or the other, or of a combination of them, depends on the objectives and nature of the social programs, the magnitude and characteristics of poverty (vulnerability), institutional factors, and the availability of timely and pertinent information. In accordance with the demand for a community approach to poverty, territorial targeting is being postulated as an important orientation for poverty programs.

Decentralization

The current democratic government aims to expand on the legacy of the military government in social policy through support for a gradual process of decentralization in the political, economic, and financial spheres. The policies adopted in support of decentralization are numerous and include the following:

- Creation of regional governments, allocation of resources for the staffing and operation of these new levels of government, and constitution of indirectly elected regional councils, with representatives from the municipal level;
- Incremental growth in the proportion of public investment governed by the regional government and council (the target is to reach 42% by 2000, but by 1996 the percentage was 26%, only 6% higher than in 1989 [Serrano 1996]);
- Constitution of democratically elected municipal councils (the first postmilitary municipal elections took place in June 1993, then in October 1996);[5]
- Development of training and technical assistance for regional governments and municipalities; and
- Improvement of financing and resource-allocation mechanisms for both health and educational establishments administered by the municipalities or the private sector.

The government also recognizes a particular need to enhance participation and community involvement and to develop linkages between decentralized government agencies and civil society if decentralization processes in general are to succeed. Measures are in place to accomplish these ends, but most of these efforts remain at a formal, legal level.

Public–private partnership

A key objective of the present government is to foster public–private partnerships in social matters. It is pursuing this objective at three levels: first, at the political level, the private sector and civil society have been explicitly invited to collaborate in formulating and designing social policies; second, at the financial level, the government has defined opportunities and incentives for the private sector and civil

---

[5] This measure, coupled with the experience accumulated by the municipalities in the previous years, contributed to the establishment of Asociación Nacional Municipal (national municipal association), an entity that is playing an important role in furthering the autonomy of the municipalities vis-à-vis the government, as well as providing information, training, and technical assistance to local administrations.

society to support social programs; and, third, at the service-provision and project-implementation level, the responsibility for design and implementation of specific projects has been transferred to subnational actors.

Overall, the goal of partnership-building is to have the state design lines of action and programs for implementation by a decentralized government agency or the private sector (for example, NGOs, social organizations, business associations, schools, universities, church associations). Toward this end, a competitive mechanism has been designed to subcontract implementation tasks. Bids from these agencies are evaluated according to quality, suitability, and cost criteria, among others. In this way, the state supports the constitution of spaces for diverse local actors to come forth with solutions to collective social problems. The instrument — the call for bids — and its implementation have not been without problems. These include dispersion and lack of coordination of effort; inadequate technical ex ante evaluation of projects; lack of experience among the implementing agencies; rigid standardization of social programs, which impedes local flexibility; inadequate supervision and monitoring of programs by new service providers; segmented and highly vertical organization of the Chilean state apparatus; and the precariousness of municipalities in heading the processes of local development (Raczynski 1998b).

The government has evaluated and tries to monitor the equity and efficiency of the systems for social security, health, and education and has taken measures to perfect these systems, strengthening the regulatory functions of the state and negotiating reform proposals, where necessary. A significant incremental reform is taking place in education, one that aims to improve the quality and equity of basic and secondary education through programs that directly affect the educational process, its financing, and the situation of teachers in state-financed private and municipal schools (Cox 1997). The government has put social-security measures in place to lower the administrative costs of the AFP system, elevate its transparency, and improve the investment possibilities for the pension funds accumulated by the AFPs. In the health sector, the situation is at an impasse. On the one hand, the increased budget allocated to the public health sector has had scant impact on the quantity and quality of health services delivered to the population (PAL 1994; Celedón and Oyarzo 1998). On the other hand, the private for-profit health investors have boycotted measures to make the ISAPRE system more transparent to the population and protect the rights of the affiliates. Government efforts to negotiate basic minimum agreements have failed, in part because of a lack of vision or direction and in part because of the government's poor strategies for communication with private health investors and medical professions.

Support for demand- over supply-driven mechanisms
The continued emphasis on demand- over supply-driven social policies and programs assumes a heightened civic responsibility and participation in social matters. Citizens and civil-society organizations are expected to define priorities, choose among alternatives, develop projects, and participate in the implementation and evaluation of programs. Yet, demand-driven mechanisms also leave an important role for the state in strengthening and qualifying demand and in ensuring that demand converges positively with supply-side forces. The recognition is growing in democratic Chile that the consequences of social policies and programs governed by demand or supply mechanisms must be monitored closely to prevent social segmentation and exclusion. For example, mechanisms used to allocate resources in the health and education sectors have been revised to introduce effective incentives to improve the quality and efficiency of services. The government is about to have an evaluation of the new rules that guide the USE mechanism in education and to implement a capitation scheme on the basis of the population enrolled at municipal health facilities.

Implementing the new approach to social policy

Given the breadth of innovations to social policies and programs introduced by Chile's democratic governments, this chapter cannot provide a comprehensive review. The range of such changes includes the creation of qualitatively new social programs; improvements to education and youth training; support for urban and rural microenterprises; and the establishment of public institutions to support policies for vulnerable groups (MIDEPLAN 1996). In 1994, a new instrument to be used in the fight against poverty was established: Fondo de Solidaridad e Inversión Social (FOSIS, social solidarity and investment fund). This program departs from the emergency and compensatory character of the majority of the Latin American social funds and defines itself as an innovative supplement to sectoral social policies and programs. Other initiatives have fostered cooperation between the private and the public sectors, whereas still others have encouraged the decentralization of social policy to regional government and local administrations.

A variety of challenges persist, however. The process of social-policy reform under Chile's democratic regimes has been hampered by numerous ambiguities and contradictions. For example, a study of Chile's antipoverty strategy completed in late 1993 analyzed the general strategy and three particularly important programs: the Chilean youth training program; the program to improve quality and equity of elementary schools, called MECE-*básica* (Mejoramiento de la Equidad y Calidad de la Educación [program for improvement of equity and quality of education–basic education]); and the program Entre Todos (all together) of FOSIS. Although Chile has a coherent and sophisticated social-policy strategy, the study (Raczynski 1995, p. 257) suggested that

> the strategy becomes diluted in the process of implementation. The result is a series of programs that are successful in achieving their short-term sectoral goals but that fail to converge, or could converge better, on their effect on poverty.

The study pointed to the fragmentation and lack of coordination among programs, as well as to a mismatch between a traditional, centralized, sectoral model of social-sector management and a decentralized, flexible, participatory one.

With regard to decentralization, the responsibilities and functions of regional governments have been defined in general terms, leaving ample room for multiple interpretations concerning national–regional–local interrelationships. Policy issues tend to be addressed at a general, rhetorical level, rather than at a concrete level. Further, among policymakers and in Congress, there is no shared understanding about the meaning, limits, and potential of decentralization. A clear and effective communication strategy – a key prerequisite for effective implementation – is also missing.

Tensions also persist between trends to centralization and decentralization. Specifically, decentralization undertaken at the administrative, political, and financial levels coexists with, and contradicts, the centralizing measures taken at the managerial level. This imposes limits and rigidities on local capacities, especially in the health and education sectors. Preparation of the national budget continues to follow the traditional, centralized, sectoral logic. Finally, this failure to decentralize effectively is grounded in, and partially explained by, the central administration's lack of faith in the capacity of regional- and local-level administrations to fulfill their new duties and manage more resources. Thus, questions of attitude and political will are playing a role in obstructing the transfer of resources and decision-making power.

Further barriers to effective social-policy reform in Chile are the technical weaknesses at the local level. Difficulties prevail at subnational levels in establishing competent and stable working teams. This is mainly because the public and private sectors compete for qualified professionals but the public sector cannot offer equivalent wages and promotion opportunities. The rotation of qualified personnel and instability of working teams also constitute significant problems at the central-government level. The difficulties at the regional and local levels are compounded by the ambiguous definition and delimitation of central-state functions and by bureaucratic resistance to the decentralization of service delivery. Also absent are methodological instruments and tools to permit the systematic monitoring of decentralization processes and to support interventions for empowerment from the central level.

Despite these obstacles, however, some progress can be acknowledged. Since 1990 regional governments have been installed and are functioning, and municipal administrations have been technically strengthened and politically democratized. Further achievements include the self-organization of local actors; the consolidation of regional governments; the development by municipalities of local participatory mechanisms; the local development of some strategic planning capacities; productive and locally unique public–private collaborative efforts; and the articulation of a culturally and socially relevant definition of poverty that emphasizes its diversity and its noneconomic dimensions (CNSP 1996). Taken together, these processes suggest the evolution of a new model of social protection.

Results and challenges: the context for social policy in Chile today

Today, Chile can point to numerous indicators of economic success, some of which date back to the last years of the military government. For the past 10 years, the annual rate of economic growth has been about 7%; inflation has been low and under control; real wages have risen; unemployment rates have fallen and fluctuated between 5% and 6% since the early 1990s; the size of the informal sector has declined; and traditional human-development indicators in health, education, and life expectancy are among the best in Latin America, and they are improving. The number of people suffering income-based poverty has fallen significantly from 5.2 million in 1990 to 3.9 million in 1994, then to 3.3 million in 1996 (MIDEPLAN n.d.). This reduction is closely related to conditions in the labour market, specifically the rate of unemployment, the creation of new jobs and income-generating opportunities, and wage trends. Around 80% of the reduction in poverty can be explained by economic growth — not unexpectedly, given the interrelationship of the economy and the labour market (Larrañaga 1994).

Although poverty has been reduced, socioeconomic inequalities have not diminished significantly. Disparities in household-income distribution are among the highest in the region: the Gini coefficient is at 0.48; the wealthiest quintile absorbs around 57% of total family income; and the lowest quintile absorbs around 4%. The family income of the highest quintile is about 11–12 times that of the lowest. In the 1970s and 1980s the distribution of income worsened, but in the 1990s it has remained relatively stable (MIDEPLAN 1996).

Public expenditures do improve the distribution of income. Yet, it is premature to conclude that they do or do not generate greater social inclusion and fairness. The social programs currently being implemented can only have significant impact over the medium and long term. The results of educational reform will be observed in the next generation; the process of decentralization is still in its early stages; and the new programs and instruments to fight poverty do not aim at immediate increases in income but at local empowerment and strengthening of assets and capacities.

In future, these types of programs are particularly important because the reduction of poverty is likely to become more difficult and more complex than in the past. Already, the rate of reduction in poverty levels has slowed. Although in 1992, Chile had 0.9 million fewer poor persons than in 1990, in 1994 it had only 0.4 million fewer poor persons than in 1992. The rate continued to decline in 1996. Reductions in poverty in 1990–92 can be attributed to factors related to the labour market, as well as to policy decisions that increased the real value of minimum income, monetary income transfers (for example, child allowances, welfare pensions), and wage levels. Since 1992 the value of these transfers has been adjusted according to inflation. Unemployment has reached its "natural," or "normal," level, making further reductions difficult. Further, it is likely that the population that overcame poverty in the early 1990s had a higher potential to do so: more education; access to more diverse support networks; and residence or work, or both, in areas with greater possibilities for development and upward mobility (Bengoa 1995). Thus, it will be more difficult to reduce poverty in the future, and empowerment-oriented antipoverty programs like those implemented in recent years will be very important. However, a critical element of their success will be the capacities for rigorous monitoring and impact evaluation, which remain underdeveloped in Chile.

Conclusions and key research issues

The design and provision of social services in Chile is entering a phase that differs from the neoliberal approach prevalent in the 1970s and 1980s, as well as from the state-dominated one prevalent during the first six decades of the century. The new approach is currently in flux: it does not rest on a shared vision, and its implementation confronts significant obstacles. However, innovative elements in the new approach can be found in the new interplay between the state, the market, and society at the national, regional, and local levels. The latest model for social development in Chile promotes autonomy among actors and agents and fosters complementarity and partnership between them and a new philosophy of governance that gives priority to grass-roots demands and strives to empower vulnerable populations. Whether and how the model will be consolidated depends on several critical factors. These include the empowerment of civil society and its organizations, including improvements to strengthen the commitment and technical capacity of NGOs and other nonprofit organizations; the development of capabilities at national, regional, and local levels to set priorities, design flexible programs, and monitor and evaluate them; and the engagement of commercial and for-profit organizations with the values of equity, social integration, and responsibility for the provision of public goods.

Some of the most important challenges also relate to the future functions and operation of the state. First, the state must assume leadership in articulating a vision, mobilizing support, setting policy priorities, and constructing flexible and innovative mechanisms to engage civil society and the private sector in the provision of public goods. A second priority for the state is to strengthen its managerial capacity. This will entail the state's being very active in its policy-setting and regulative role but limiting its traditional responsibility for direct provision of services and execution of programs. Third, the state must strengthen its role in monitoring and evaluating social policies and develop instruments to support this. So far, little has been done in this respect, and the methodological challenge is enormous. Decentralization and public–private partnerships can only be made compatible with equity if the state adopts systematic mechanisms to monitor results and evaluate the social impacts of the reforms. Fourth, the state must make efforts to diminish the incongruence between its own traditional, sectoral, vertical organization and the requirements of decentralization, community involvement, and public–private partnerships. This requires flexibility in programs and procedures and participatory decision-making processes that encourage collective strategic planning among actors at the local level. Finally, the state must make genuine efforts to ensure community involvement and social participation without reducing these to mere formal or juridical processes of participation, as has usually been the case. A particular effort must be made to sensitize the nonpoor and institutional actors to work both with and for the poor.

The Chilean experience is rich with policy lessons. Some of these lessons have been highlighted above. The following is a list of research issues that are of outstanding importance. These issues occur at four levels; the first two are directly relevant to policy-making, and the latter two are more academic but have important policy implications.

Program design, implementation, and evaluation

The list of key research issues relating to program design, implementation and evaluation includes

- Monitoring and evaluation of social programs and improved collection of relevant information, particularly regarding beneficiaries and the changes that beneficiaries or the communities, or both, undergo as a consequence of social programs;

- Identification of common bottlenecks in the design and implementation of social programs and recommendations for the improvement of these processes;

- Evaluation of the capacity of public social programs to reach different communities and identification of the means to make these programs more accommodating and responsive to local organizations and groups; and

- Evaluation of the strengths and weaknesses of a territorial approach to poverty, as opposed to one that centres on categories of the population, and development of policy instruments appropriate for use with a territorial approach (for example, community assessments, strategic planning, monitoring, evaluation).

Institutional frameworks

The important issues relating to institutional frameworks include

- Analysis of decentralization processes, with special attention to national–regional–local relations, functions of agents at each level, incentive structures, linkages between political and technical aspects in decision-making, issues of participation and accountability, and the means of strengthening policy design, regulation, and evaluation at the national level; and

- Examination of the interrelationship between public and private sectors in the formulation, design, implementation, and evaluation of social programs.

Compatibility between market principles and social equity

The key issues for research relating to compatibility between market principles and social equity include

- Analysis of the relationship between economic growth, labour-market conditions, capital accumulation, and social policies; and

- Identification of the challenges for social and labour policy presented by national integration and participation in the global economy.

Current social-welfare model and social structure

Important issues relating to the current social-welfare model and social structure include

- Identification of the main characteristics of the society and social-welfare structure currently emerging in Chile;
- Evaluation of how effectively the country is building a new model of social well-being that points toward equity and social integration;
- Identification of the central actors in the system and the main axes of conflict;
- Analysis of the ways the new actors are evolving;
- Evaluation of how well the citizens' voices and demands are incorporated into the system; and
- Identification of emerging social vulnerabilities and the ways society and social policy respond to these.

Annex A. Models of social protection in Chile, 1970 to 1990s.

Dimensions	Traditional state-dominated model	Neoliberal model	Emergent model
Economic–social policy	Weak relationship; fiscal imbalance	Social policy subordinated to economic policy; fiscal balance achieved mainly by cuts in expenditures	Social policy integrated with, and complementary to, economic policy; fiscal balance looking both at revenues and expenditures
Goal–purpose–function of social policies	Nation-state building, industrialization, social integration	Poverty alleviation, satisfaction of basic needs of the poor	Growth with equity, social integration, poverty reduction
Policy content and orientation	Supply and coverage of social services (education, health, social security, housing); standardized programs and procedures; absence of adaptation to regional or local conditions Protective labour legislation Price subsidies for basic consumer goods	Supply of basic social services for the poor; reach directed to poverty pockets; special poverty-alleviation programs (safety nets); standardized programs and procedures Minimum of labour regulation; maximum of flexibility for the firm Privatization of social security and social services for the nonpoor	Equity and quality of education and health Reach directed to poverty pockets with programs that support capabilities and opportunities (youth training, urban and rural small productive activities, support to community organizations, and social participation); adaptation of program content and methodology to the diversity of poverty situations Labour regulations that protect labour mobility
Roles of the state, market, and civil society	State dominance (formulates, regulates, finances, delivers social services and programs) Little space for private markets or for community initiatives	State designs, regulates, and finances programs for the poor; privatization of social services for the nonpoor and administration and delivery of state-financed services for the poor by the private sector and local units of the state	"State plus civil society"; strategic or catalytic role of the state with emphasis on policy setting, regulation, and monitoring and evaluation functions; state also contributes to financing services and may, under special circumstances, deliver services, preferably in a decentralized form
Centralization–decentralization	Centralized	Centralized national programs oriented to the poor; deconcentration of education and health services	Deepening of decentralization at the political, technical, and social-participation dimensions

(continued)

Annex A concluded.

Dimensions	Traditional state-dominated model	Neoliberal model	Emergent model
Logic of decision-making	Bureaucratic; state dominance, with heavy influence of corporate interests and groups; centrality of political considerations; top-down decision-making	Incorporation of technical–analytic and economic considerations; top-down decision-making	Incorporation of technical–analytic and economic considerations; development of instruments for regional and local decision-making, community participation, and public–private collaboration
Financing	General and specific taxes, plus worker and employer mandatory social-security and health contributions	Taxes and worker mandatory social-security and health contributions; state finances only services for the poor; cost recovery	Taxes and workers mandatory social-security and health contributions; state finances basic social services for the population; cost recovery
Allocation of public resources — supply and demand	Supply-driven mechanisms; historic allocation trends	Introduction of demand-driven mechanisms; allocation according to poverty indexes	Combination of demand- and supply-driven mechanisms, which vary, depending on the objectives of specific programs; allocation according to poverty indexes in some programs
Level and trends in public expenditures	Growing	As low as possible, depending on the size of the poor population and fiscal balance	No definite trend; fiscal balance is central and can be obtained through less spending and more revenues

Source: from Raczynski (1997) and ECLAC (1995).

Chapter 4

Canada

Experience and Lessons for the Future

Terrance Hunsley

Social policy has traditionally been driven by domestic economic, demographic, and political concerns. However, in recent years, economic globalization has added a new and powerful set of conditions and forces that have influenced public-policy agendas and decision-making. To what extent the new global context has come to dominate national social policy is a question that merits serious consideration, as the emergence of the global economy has coincided with a broad range of activities to reformulate social policies and institutional social systems. It would seem that processes of social-policy reform in several countries and regions are taking the same general path as the globalization of the economy.

Because Canada is a country considered "developed," in the lexicon of international comparison, and currently occupies a top position on the United Nations Development Programme's (UNDP's) Human Development Index (HDI) (UNDP 1997), it may be useful to explore whether its social-policy reform is following a trajectory similar to that being observed in other countries and regions.

In this chapter, social policy is understood as the responsibility of the nation-state

- To provide necessary structures for collective security and appropriate collective consumption (social insurance, health care, education);
- To establish and enforce principles of access and equity in the conduct of public and private affairs;
- To alleviate hardship and disadvantage through ensuring basic living standards; and
- To foster the development of a healthy, adaptable, competent, cohesive, and successful population.

The shared well-being of national populations, the cooperation necessary for collective adaptation to changing national and international environments, and the social policies that advance these concerns might be the "social glue" essential for nation-states to succeed in the next century.

In light of these considerations, this chapter describes the process and content of recent social-policy reform in Canada. It argues that Canada's privileged economic position, its relatively young demographic structure (compared with other rich countries), its established welfare state, and the diffused institutional structure of social-policy decision-making have caused, or allowed, it to adapt social policies relatively slowly. To go a step further, this chapter postulates that social-policy changes in Canada between 1980 and 1990 have resembled fiscal conservatism more than reform and have been more a response to a decrease in public confidence in government than a response to any paradigm shift in social-policy theory. In the past 5 years, however, the processes of change have accelerated. Characteristics of a new policy configuration are beginning to emerge with more consistency, a defining characteristic of systemic reform.

It is argued that a nation that has opened its economy to global trade requires more sophisticated forms of social protection and development. The numbers and varieties of actors in the social-policy mix are increasing; the factors of both demand and supply are in constant flux. Public policy therefore faces increasingly complex challenges.

This chapter begins with an economic, demographic, and institutional profile of Canada. This is followed by a discussion of the evolution of Canadian social policy and a description of the reform initiatives that have preoccupied social policymakers during the 1980s and 1990s. The likely directions of social policy in the years to come are especially emphasized. This chapter concludes with observations on the significance of the reforms and on global and domestic influences on social-policy decisions. In this context, suggestions are provided for the direction of future collaborative international research.

A national profile

Socioeconomic trends

Canada is a vast nation with a low population density. Its 28 million people occupy only a small portion of the land mass. Although it is a middle power in the international geopolitical context, Canada is among the richer nations of the world. The gross domestic product (GDP) per capita was about 25% lower than that of the United States in 1995 but roughly equal to those of Japan and Germany.[1] Canada's active role in international affairs has secured it membership in the Group of Seven. Although Canada trades globally, its major trading partner has historically been the United States, and its relationship with the United States strongly influences Canada's domestic policies. A major public-policy concern during the latter half of the 1980s was securing a free-trade agreement with the United States, as Canadian political leaders feared that increased US protectionism could be disastrous to the Canadian economy.

During the 1980s and 1990s, Canada experienced relatively steady economic growth. Table 1 shows that despite two recessions, gross national product per capita grew in Canada at an average annual rate of 2.2% from 1980 to 1993, only 0.2% below that of the United States and higher than those of Denmark, France, the Netherlands, Sweden, and the United Kingdom.

Canada is among the more indebted of the wealthy nations. In 1993, the national debt was equal to 92.2% of GDP. This situation

---

[1] Policy Research Committee. 1996. Growth, human development, social cohesion. Government of Canada, Ottawa. Draft interim report. Unpublished.

Table 1. Comparisons of national debt and economic growth, 1980–93.

Country	Debt as % GDP, 1993	Average annual growth in GNP per capita, 1980–93 (%)
Australia	33.3	2.7
Canada	92.2	2.2
Denmark	142.2	1.8
France	52.2	1.8
Germany	50.2	2.8
Netherlands	79.2	1.9
Norway	44.8	2.6
Sweden	83.5	0.9
United Kingdom	47.1	2.0
United States	64.3	2.4

Source: UNDP (1993b, 1997).
Note: GDP, gross domestic product; GNP, gross national product.

fueled political pressure to reduce operating deficits, with the result that expenditures on social programs became a national concern. In the past few years, the federal operating deficit has been brought under control and current projections indicate that the federal government is on the verge of achieving a surplus operating budget.

Provincial government budgets are a mix of surpluses and deficits. These governments have been experiencing their own budget pressures. Although the major portion of the costs of income-security programs are federal, recent decisions have begun shifting more of this responsibility to the provincial governments. The provincial governments were already struggling with rising costs of health care and education, and they now bear most of the costs of poverty alleviation.

Despite Canada's growing economy, unemployment has become a major social and economic problem. Official unemployment rates have hovered around 10% over the past 10 years, but unofficial estimates of real unemployment are much higher. Official rates of unemployment may not include people who are unemployed but not actively seeking employment or those who are working part-time while seeking full-time work. Official rates also disregard periods of lack of income among the self-employed.

Canada has also experienced an increase in income inequality, especially in labour-market incomes. The social-security system has been hard put to maintain relative stability in the distribution of after-tax family incomes. Income disparity among individuals has increased, especially disparities between older and younger adults. The number of people dependent on social transfers has roughly doubled since 1980 (Hunsley 1992).

In sum, increases in unemployment and in the proportion of lower-paying jobs have resulted in lower tax revenues and increased pressure on income-related programs and employment insurance, at a time when fiscal deficits have become a major political concern.

Sociodemographic perspectives

Like most of the Organisation for Economic Co-operation and Development (OECD) nations, Canada is experiencing population aging. The population over the age of 65 years is increasing steadily. The smaller population over the age of 75 years is growing much more rapidly and is of concern for social policy because of the public costs involved for health care and income support and other social-support services. The aging population is a political concern because of the projected liabilities accruing to younger generations for support of people who are retiring earlier than before. Benefits are based on wages that are higher than those of the younger generation and will be paid out for a longer time than anticipated when the public pension system was put in place 30 years ago.

Nevertheless, as Table 2 illustrates, Canada's population aging is not as advanced as in many other nations, and this is a result of one of the greatest baby booms in all countries after World War II. The baby-boom phenomenon, combined with a rapid increase in female participation in the labour force in the 1960s and 1970s, has created a very favourable ratio of labour force to economically dependent population. Moreover, although fertility rates have fallen by half in the postwar years, the large cohort of baby-boomer parents has produced a supply of children about equal to the projected number of those who will leave the labour force over the next 15 years. So the full economic impact of population aging is being delayed and mitigated by the large numbers of young people and by the increased labour-market activity of women.

On an international scale, the quality of life in Canada is among the highest of all nations. Canada has several times occupied the number-one rating on the UNDP HDI (1995–97), although the ranking falls several points when the gender-adjusted index is used. This suggests that Canada's favourable combination of health, education,

Table 2. Demographic and social characteristics.

Country	% of population over age 65, 1994	Income-inequality ratio, 1980–94[a]	Demographic-dependency ratio, 1994[b]	Labour-force replacement ratio, 1994[c]
Australia	11.7	9.58	49.8	103
Canada	11.9	7.05	47.9	97
Denmark	15.2	7.15	48.1	82
France	14.9	7.48	52.8	97
Germany	15.2	5.77	45.6	76
Netherlands	13.1	4.50	45.8	86
Norway	16.0	5.92	54.4	95
Sweden	17.4	4.61	56.3	94
United Kingdom	15.8	9.65	54.1	96
United States	12.6	8.91	53.2	108

Note: GDP, gross domestic product.

[a] The ratio of the GDP per capita of richest 20% of the population to that of the poorest 20%.

[b] The ratio of the population of people more than 65 years of age and less than 16 years of age to that of people who are economically active.

[c] The ratio of the population of people less than 16 years of age to that of people between the ages of 45 and 64 years.

and income status is not shared as equitably on a gender basis as in other countries. International comparative research focusing on income distribution (Smeeding 1996; Hunsley 1997a) also pointed out that Canada — like Australia, the United Kingdom, and the United States — has more income inequality than several European countries. This entails higher proportions of low-income people in the population. These countries are typified as having "liberal" or "residual" welfare states (Esping-Anderson 1990), which rely on income-tested relief for the long-term unemployed and poor, rather than demogrant[2] programs and more active state intervention in the labour market.

Political-institutional characteristics

Canada is made up of former colonies of Britain and France. It functions with many of the traditional structures of the British Parliamentary system. Quebec, which was originally a French colony, retains several distinctive features in its educational and judicial systems. Quebec is one of 10 provinces and 3 territories in the federation, and it contains roughly one-quarter of the population. The Quebec

---

[2] A universal cash grant of some specified amount per person.

legal system is based on the French Civil Code, whereas the rest of the country uses the common law. Quebec has traditionally chosen to exercise options to maximize provincial jurisdiction and delivery of social programs and consequently has a more complete and distinctive social-policy structure than do other provinces.

Canadian domestic politics has historically reflected a need to constantly broker arrangements to respond to the divergent aspirations of its geographically and culturally diverse people. Regional differences have been especially evident in the long-standing struggle in Quebec between prosovereignty and federalist groups. Quebec nationalism has given added impetus to provincial demands for broader jurisdictions. The "Quebec situation" has become a dominant factor in federal government decisions. Two major efforts of federal and provincial leaders during the 1980s to shift more power to Quebec and other provinces ended in political failure when the proposed accords (the Meech Lake Accord and the Charlottetown Accord) were rejected by specific provincial legislatures or by public referendum. These accords were intended to amend the *Constitution Act* to limit the capacity of the federal government to spend money (with associated conditionality) in areas of provincial jurisdiction and would have shifted the responsibility for adult occupational training to the provinces. The constitutional basis for federal involvement in adult training was vague in any case. Despite the fact that neither of these accords was adopted, the prevailing political impetus in federal-provincial arrangements moves in the direction of continued decentralization, albeit within current constitutional provisions.

Canadian provincial governments are not subordinate to the federal government. The *Constitution Act*, which replaced the *British North America Act*, assigns specific powers exclusively to each order of government. It places most of the responsibility for social programs in the provincial domain, under the categories of hospitals, schools, local matters, and charitable institutions. As a result, provinces have jurisdiction over health, education, most labour matters, poverty alleviation, social services, and municipal governments. However, the federal government has predominant taxing powers. It was first to enter the income-tax field and is authorized to levy customs and excise taxes, taxes at any stage of production or distribution of goods and services, and payroll deductions for social insurance. It also holds residual powers through its responsibility for "peace, order and good government," a clause in the *Constitution Act* that is often cited as characteristic of Canadian values, in contrast to the US provisions for individual freedoms and the "pursuit of happiness." The tendency has been for the provinces to be restricted to a secondary role in income taxes, retail sales taxes, property taxes, royalties on natural-resource extraction, social-insurance premiums, and various types of licences and fees.

The federal government has the power to spend money in any area, so long as it does not interfere with provincial authority. Federal funds have been used in social policy, either to assist provincial programs (with associated conditions) or to intervene directly when provinces agree to enabling constitutional arrangements. Such arrangements now exist in respect to unemployment insurance, old-age pensions, and the Canada/Quebec Pension Plan. The federal government operates unemployment insurance and old-age pensions exclusively, whereas the Canada/Quebec Pension Plan is operated under a combined federal–provincial authority. Under the latter agreement, the provinces retain the right to preempt the federal program by operating their own, so long as it is compatible with the federal one. Thus far, only Quebec has exercised this option (hence the name of the program).

Federal transfers for children through the Child Tax Benefit were originally upheld by the Supreme Court (when they were called Family Allowances) as a legitimate exercise of spending power. The federal government is involved in health and post-secondary education through transfers to provincial governments. The funds for health care are subject to a set of principles negotiated at the time the funds were established and then drafted into law by the federal government.

The Constitution has other provisions that relate to federal-provincial arrangements and social policy. They include the Equalization Clause and the *Charter of Rights and Freedoms*.

In this context, *equalization* refers, first, to the objective, articulated in the *Constitution Act*, of federal and provincial governments' working to reduce economic disparities among regions and provide in all regions public services of "reasonably comparable" quality at "reasonably comparable" levels of taxation. Second, the Equalization Clause refers to the program established to pursue the latter objective through federal government transfers from its tax base, with formula-defined funds directed to lower-revenue provinces. Although the status of some provinces may change from time to time, depending on their economic performance, at least half of the provinces are usually receiving equalization payments from the federal government.

The *Charter of Rights and Freedoms* is adjoined to the Constitution and provides protection for Canadian residents in their relationship with government, rather than in their relationship to each other — provincial governments are responsible for most human-rights legislation. Among other provisions, the Charter prohibits discriminatory treatment on a number of specified grounds, such as gender or race, as well as unspecified grounds. A group does not have to be specified to enjoy the protection of the Charter. It applies to individual and systemic discrimination and includes the concept of equal benefit of the law. This concept allows plaintiffs to challenge government programs not only on the basis of equality of access but also on the basis of measured systemic outcomes. For provinces not to be subject to the Charter, they have to declare themselves to be doing something "notwithstanding" the provisions of the Charter, an action that would guarantee political unpopularity.

The federal government also becomes engaged in social policy because it is responsible for foreign affairs. This includes negotiating reciprocal social-security arrangements with other countries. It also includes ratification and operational protocols of international treaties, such as free-trade agreements and the United Nations conventions.

The trade agreements influence social policies by establishing conditions for private business to operate, reducing tariffs that protect domestic jobs, and establishing rules of competition for provision of publicly subsidized services. They also place limits on the development of public monopolies, which have often been the instrument of delivering social insurance.

The United Nations conventions are for the most part unenforceable in Canadian courts because they have not been written into domestic law and because the Constitution does not define any status for them. There are a few instances where conventions (for example, on the abduction of children) are replicated in provincial law and become enforceable. Although most conventions are unenforceable in Canada, they are standards with moral credibility in the country and indirectly influence domestic policies. When a United Nations agency criticizes Canadian policies for not fulfilling the obligations of a convention it has signed, the government usually attempts to rectify the problem. This was the case, for example, in the 1980s when Quebec acted to amend a controversial law restricting the commercial use of the English language, after the law was criticized as discriminatory by a United Nations body.

Sociopolitical traditions

Organized groups promote their interests at all stages of the legislative process in Canada. The more powerful business and professional organizations exert more influence; however, popular groups may also be effective, depending on the situation. Labour is organized at federal and provincial levels and actively attempts to influence policy. In recent years, the influence of organized labour appears to have decreased. During the 1970s, the federal government espoused a policy of pluralism and actively assisted social-interest groups to form national associations to participate in the policy-development process. As a result, national social-interest organizations actively promote their agendas with the federal government.

At different periods, the influence of specific social interests may grow and recede. In the early 1980s, the expansion of women's organizations gave them a prominent role in many policy issues. A federal agency to promote the status of women was instituted, and a prominent national women's organization was accorded a unique annual privilege of meeting with a large group of cabinet ministers. Recently, organizations representing the interests of older citizens are gaining more political influence. In general, however, the influence of national social-interest organizations has decreased in recent decades, and their grants from the federal government have decreased dramatically. At the provincial level, the organization of social interests is less advanced, although the picture varies from province to province. Labour and professional associations are active at provincial levels because they are more likely to be concerned directly with provincial legislation.

In all, civil society plays an active role in policy-making. As well, many provinces use nonprofit organizations to deliver public services. The nonprofit sector is also organized to raise funds for the support of community-based services that governments are not prepared or able to provide. The balance of public and private services has shifted over time, but until 1980 it was gradually becoming more government dominated. During the 1980s, a discernible shift took place in delivery policies, and the nonprofit sector began to grow again.

For most of Canada's history, two national parties, the Liberals and Conservatives, have dominated politics at both federal and provincial levels. Both parties compete for the middle of the political spectrum, which, according to the popular media, has itself been drifting to the right for two decades. A third national party, social democratic in orientation, has occasionally held the balance of power nationally and has formed the government for varying periods in a few provinces. Two major regional parties have grown up in the past decade. One of these parties represents separatist interests in Quebec, and the other is a right-wing party strongly based in western Canada. The change in political balance has coincided with and reinforced a general momentum to shift more power to provincial governments.

The roles of municipal governments in Canada have been growing steadily in recent years. Although municipal governments are created by and directly answerable to provincial governments, they have been seeking a more powerful role in national governance. In several provinces, the larger municipal governments have a role in the delivery of social programs. They may also contribute to financing them, although this is a still a minor municipal role in the overall pattern of social policy.

The evolution of Canadian social policy

The development of Canadian social policy mirrors the economic and political history of the country during the 20th century. During the first four decades of this century, Canada's new industrial economy changed the lifestyles of the people, and provisions were needed to ensure society would be mobile, with people traveling to the cities and other locations where jobs were available. Cities were built on manufacturing economies; remote sites were developed for resource extraction. The employees were mostly men, and their wives moved with them. New family units appeared, often far from the extended family.

During this phase, provincial and municipal governments, churches, and community organizations provided assistance to the poor, the disabled, and orphans. The first forms of social insurance were workers' compensation programs for injured workers, beginning in 1912. Modest income-security programs for the elderly, veterans, and widows were introduced during the 1920s. Local governments provided last-resort social-assistance programs with limited assistance from provincial governments, and when jobs were scarce, some provinces established short-term work projects to help the unemployed.

In the 1930s, the Great Depression exposed the weakness of the existing social-protection programs. Local governments were financially incapable of continuing even modest levels of public assistance. Municipal and provincial governments were small operations, and taxation was much less extensive than today. Consequently, these governments were incapable of meeting people's needs for assistance.

The critical stimulus for a modern social-policy system came from the need to rebuild a peacetime economy after World War II. At that time, the role of the federal government was in ascendency, in part because of the centralization of the power of taxation, which had been introduced to support the war effort. Encouraged by a strong sense of national identity, the federal government engaged provincial governments in discussions of new national programs. A Royal Commission (Rowell–Sirois) to review federal–provincial arrangements recommended that Canada establish an integrated social-security system. Over the next 30 years, programs were introduced to provide medical and unemployment insurance, occupational and age-related pensions, and improved social-assistance benefits. They were either financed directly by the federal government (such as Family Allowances and Unemployment Insurance) or cost-shared with provincial governments (such as Blind Persons Allowances, Disabled Persons Allowances, income-tested Unemployment Assistance, and Hospital Insurance and Diagnostic Services).

Although these developments were an intervention of the federal government in areas of provincial jurisdiction, the provinces were for the most part supportive of the changes and recognized the need to provide social supports for the new economic system. Gaining provincial agreement often required federal acceptance of some or all of the costs. With financial assistance from the federal government, provinces were able to expand and improve their existing programs or develop new ones.

In turn, the federal government usually insisted on some form of national consistency in guiding principles. In some cases, it achieved this through the specific conditions it attached to the provinces' claiming cost-sharing funds. These conditions tended to be administrative criteria, rather than standards. For example, they specified the particular cost items to be shared. In the case of social assistance one of the conditions was that provinces apply a test of need to applicants for financial assistance. Although this test of need limited federal liability, it also became, in operation, a form of entitlement to people who met the criteria set out in the needs test.

In later years, the federal government moved away from cost-sharing models to predetermined block transfers. In health care, the federal government specified a set of guiding principles for the provinces to respect in return for federal funds. In total, the process achieved national consistency in the form and extent of social protection across the country, even if the specific conditions of eligibility, extent of benefits, and generosity of those benefits varied in accordance with provincial priorities and fiscal capacities. Although the federal government steered provincial priorities by offering financial incentives, provincial governments retained a substantial degree of flexibility in the planning and development of programs.

This period of growth is often referred to as a time of cooperative federalism. It was also a period in which the social-policy process was referred to as incrementalism. This meant that the Canadian welfare state was constructed gradually. Every few years, often before elections, a new or increased benefit for a politically popular group would be offered. Then, as time passed, smaller incremental benefits would be provided to other groups so as not to create large inequities. The elderly were often the beneficiaries of improvements from the late 1950s until the late 1970s, and poverty among the elderly dropped dramatically during that period.

During the 30 years following World War II, the Canadian economy grew rapidly, and the expenditures on social programs did not result in deficit financing. The increasing level of social spending paralleled the increasing role of government in managing a national economy. Social programs had a stabilizing and moderating influence during economic fluctuations, as expenditures on programs such as Unemployment Insurance and social assistance tend to be counter-cyclical. They assisted a new society of mobile nuclear families, which might in earlier economies have been supported by extended-family structures. They also ensured a healthy and educated labour force and a peaceful society.

An interesting feature of social policies during this period is that legislation for the new programs was developed by federal and provincial officials who also participated in the elaboration of related international (United Nations) conventions. The indirect and subtle influence of this involvement in Canadian national programs was important, as federal and provincial governments have always had difficulty reaching agreement on what standards should guide social programs and on what forms of accountability should be imposed. The international conventions provided a reference point and shared learning process.

By the mid-1970s, Canada was spending more than 20% of GDP on social programs (OECD n.d.), which was still below the levels of expenditure on social programs in many other OECD countries. Canadian social programs were not as extensive or as generous as those in several European countries; however, the Canadian programs were more extensive and generous than those in the United States, Canada's major trading partner. The major differences with the United States were evident in Canada's higher levels of unemployment insurance, universal family allowances, universal medicare, and the Canadian equalization program. An important result was that Canadian workers and their families were more protected from economic fluctuations than those in the United States and were able to demand higher wages relative to output, especially at the lower end of the wage scale. This protection was supported by customs and excise taxes and by a free-floating Canadian dollar, which tended to keep prices of imported and exported goods in balance. The higher level of social protection has been a constant source of stress on the Canadian social-policy system, as Canadian firms tend to complain that they could be more competitive in US markets if they did not have to pay the higher taxes needed to support social benefits. In the debates over free trade in the 1980s, another view of the impact of Canadian social policies emerged. US negotiators pointed out that the Canadian health-care system, financed through general tax revenues, improved the competitive position of Canadian firms, as their US competitors paid for workers' health insurance as part of the wage package.

Canadian programs represented a mix of individualist and collectivist philosophies and a mix of guiding principles, delivery systems, and financing methods. Income-security programs, for example, provided both universal demogrants and income-tested benefits. The medicare system was based on universal coverage, with public financing and private delivery. Old-age security was provided through a universal age-related demogrant and an income-related supplement.

Family Allowances were provided through a universal benefit and an income-related supplement. Because of the mix of systems, Canadian governments have been able to alter the mix of universal and targeted programs over time without major reforms of the system. However, the system mix can become complicated because of the various combinations and interactions of 1 federal, 10 provincial, and 3 territorial systems, each being complex in itself.

Until the early 1980s, social protection was structured in three layers: a basic universal benefit, an income-tested supplement, and provision for individuals or employers to purchase a third layer of protection from the private market. In some cases, a tax deduction on the private expenditure assisted the latter provision.

Most programs were financed through general government revenues. Unemployment Insurance was financed through payroll deductions, as was the occupational pension program. Many public services were provided under contract with private nonprofit agencies. Others were provided directly by government employees. The mix could vary from province to province. For example, in some provinces the state delivers child-welfare services (child protection), and in others, nonprofit agencies, usually called the Children's Aid Society, deliver this service. Residential and home-care services for the elderly may vary in the same way from province to province. Where nongovernmental organizations (NGOs) deliver services, the financial support may still be primarily from government, but often a portion is generated through charitable donations, as well as through payments from the service consumers. Given that charitable donations are also state subsidized, because they provide a tax deduction for the donor, the bottom line is usually that the state is the predominant funder. The particular mix tends to reflect the social philosophy of the provincial government in question.

In general, the growth of the Canadian social-policy system in this period reflected, and responded to, the economic and social realities of the country's history. Policymakers devoted much of their attention to maintaining a balance of policies and programs to serve both local and national interests. The diversity of the country and the relatively small population occupying a large land mass seemed to require a substantial, at times cumbersome, role for national government. The complex structure of social policy that evolved reflects the country's decentralized nature. Programs were added over time in response to the growth of needs and concerns. This does not necessarily mean that the federal government always took the lead in Canadian social policy. Many new programs, including medicare, were first tested in one or more provinces, before being adopted nationally. Despite the patchwork nature of the system, the paucity of clear statements of standards of service, and the variation in generosity of benefits from province to province, most Canadians would have rightly perceived that the same basic social protections were available in one form or another across the country.

A paradigm shift? Social-policy reform from 1980 to the present

In retrospect, a thorough review of the role and financing of social programs would have been appropriate in the early 1980s. The social and demographic evolution of Canadian society had resulted in a growing demand for social protection and for support services. An aging population required a different mix of programs. The 1960s and 1970s had witnessed a dramatic transformation of the typical family structure, from one earner plus homemaker to two earners purchasing homemaking-replacement products and services. Two-earner families needed a more extensive formal support system than one-earner families, especially without the support of extended family relationships, as was increasingly the case. Increasing cultural and social diversity in the population presented challenges to community support systems that reflected the sociodemographic characteristics and norms of an earlier era. So it would have been appropriate and normal to review and reform Canada's social policies.

However, social-policy reform did not take place under normal conditions. Like other nations, Canada was swept into the new era by the global forces of political and economic transformation.

In the late 1970s economic growth slowed appreciably, whereas inflation increased. The average annual growth in GDP decreased to 2.6% between 1980 and 1993, compared with 4.6% between 1970 and 1980 (World Bank 1995b). Unemployment grew rapidly, attaining an equilibrium between 9 and 10%, compared with 6–7% in the earlier decade. By the 1990s the number of social-assistance recipients had doubled that of the 1970s (Hunsley 1992).

Early in the 1980s, it became apparent that the downturn in the Canadian economy was not a normal, cyclical one but the result of deep structural problems. Canadian labour found itself at a competitive disadvantage relative to investment in labour-saving technology. To some extent, labour became commodified for purchase on an as-needed basis. High levels of unemployment continued in the form of long-lasting structural unemployment. Large barriers to secure employment faced a young generation overshadowed politically and outweighed in seniority by their parents, and young people's wages dropped precipitously. The wage structure became polarized, with high wages at the top for those with secure employment in large institutions and for new professionals and entrepreneurs in the emerging industries and low wages for displaced or less competitive workers employed in the growing service industries.

A decade of profound economic restructuring transformed the Canadian economy. Evolving rapidly from a resource-extraction and manufacturing economy, Canadian industry became thoroughly integrated into the new order of global corporate structures and integrated production, financing, and marketing systems. Canada dismantled its tariffs on trade with the United States and Mexico and pursued other free-trade arrangements. Canadian fiscal policies pushed interest rates up to battle inflation and attract foreign capital, but the price was exacerbated unemployment.

Governments were running serious deficits and looking for ways to limit spending without causing social and economic damage. Because social programs constitute a major portion of government spending, they became a central focus in the search for ways to limit spending. During the 1980s and early 1990s, governments of all political stripes tried to restrain or reduce social-program expenditures and articulate a leaner social-policy theory. This translated into the policy shifts described below.

Policy changes at the federal level

At the federal level, policy changes included the following:

- Taxes on production and international trade (such as the manufacturing tax) were reduced or eliminated and replaced by increased consumption (goods and services) taxes. These increases were partially offset by tax credits, such as the Goods and Services Tax Credit given to low-income people.

- A major trend was the move away from universality as a desirable social-policy objective. Universal programs gradually came to be considered wasteful for providing benefits to people who "did not really need them." Even though universal benefits were treated as taxable income and had been thereby reduced for higher income people several years earlier, the recurrent trend was toward giving benefits to people with low incomes or with exceptional needs. Demogrant programs, such as Family Allowances and Old Age Security, were gradually transformed into income-tested programs.

- Concurrent with targeting was a trend to use the tax system to deliver social benefits. The revenue department collects extensive income-related information on most adults in Canada, as well as details on their assets and family situations. It is an efficient system for determining eligibility and adjusting benefits according to income. Moreover, using tax credits and refundable tax credits, as well as tax deductions, the system can achieve any desired degree of income redistribution.

- Several reductions were made in Unemployment Insurance benefits. A series of discrete initiatives over the past decade reduced the portion of earnings replaced by Unemployment Insurance, as well as the duration of insurance benefits. Eligibility was tightened by requiring more weeks of insurable employment as a prerequisite and by delaying or denying benefits to people who voluntarily leave their jobs. The benefits themselves were income targeted: a surtax was placed on benefits received in families with above-average incomes. As result, the Employment Insurance fund (as it is now known) is now running a substantial surplus, despite continuing high levels of unemployment.

- In the 1980s, worker displacement, fear of occupational obsolescence, reduced Unemployment Insurance benefits, and general stress in the workplaces coincided with a rapid increase in demand for long-term disability benefits. The

Canada Pension Plan Disability benefits program doubled its annual expenditures within a decade. By the end of the decade, tighter eligibility criteria and more frequent reviews of case files slowed the caseload increases.

- The federal government reduced financial transfers to support provincial government health, post-secondary education, and social-assistance programs. Reductions announced in the 1995 federal budget decreased transfers by about 25%, in addition to cuts in previous years. The financial transfers are a combination of cash and tax "points" (taxing power). The gradually increasing value of tax points partially offsets the reduced cash transfers.

- Some social-interest groups were able to pursue their objectives through the equality provisions of the *Charter of Rights and Freedoms*. Although governments attempted to restrain the growth of expenditures, the overall coverage of a few programs was extended by the courts or by legislative provisions to make the programs consistent with the Charter. This was the case in the extension of pension and health-insurance benefits to homosexual partners of workers and in the extension of Unemployment Insurance coverage to people more than 65 years of age.

Policy changes at the provincial level

At the provincial level, policy shifts have resulted in spending constraints in health care and in social-assistance programs, workers' compensation programs, and post-secondary education:

- Several institutions have achieved savings by imposing efficiency measures, especially in reducing stays in hospital for routine operations. Patients are discharged as soon as possible into the care of their families, usually assisted by services in the home and outpatient services. In residential institutions for people with mental and physical disabilities, rigorous deinstitutionalization policies move people rapidly into community care facilities or attempt to support their care in the home. In some cases, drug therapy has replaced surgical procedures.

- Social-assistance benefits for people considered employable have been reduced in many jurisdictions, and all provinces have introduced programs to encourage social-assistance recipients to find jobs. Because of the generally depressed labour market for people without specialized skills and because of the low pay and precarious nature of available employment, these programs have had very limited success. Provincial governments have expressed frustration with the fact that the federal government has generally controlled adult training. Negotiations are currently under way to transfer this responsibility to the provinces so that these programs might be more closely integrated with measures to reduce social-assistance caseloads.

- Much effort has been devoted to finding alternatives to government assistance for vulnerable groups. For example, in recent years child poverty has become an issue, and single-parent families are a particular focus. When parents are separated or divorced in Canada, it is not uncommon to find a pattern of failure by noncustodial parents to fulfill their obligations to help support their children. As a consequence, many single parents, especially women, find it necessary to apply for social-assistance benefits. Efforts were made to improve the enforcement of child-support payments as an alternative to government assistance.

- Because many public services are delivered by public employees, the wages of these groups have also been a focus for savings. Most public servants have experienced periods of wage freezes or reductions, and several governments have instituted "buy-out" packages and early retirement to reduce their labour force.

The Social Security Review

In 1994, the federal government announced a formal review of social-security programs. It put an extensive consultation process in place, including the appointment of a high-level advisory committee to the Minister of Human Resources Development, with representatives from academia and NGOs and nongovernmental associations with an interest in social and economic policy. A parliamentary committee was mandated to hold public hearings and to make recommendations for reform. The objectives were to make the existing system more effective, more in tune with present-day needs, and more supportive of employment but also to restrain or reduce overall expenditures. To intervene in child poverty also became an early priority.

A number of internal studies were commissioned by a team of federal officials brought together to support the exercise. For about a year the Social Security Review was a high-profile exercise that generated optimism for a broad-ranging, positively oriented reform process. Unfortunately, early in 1995, the exercise was officially curtailed, when the Finance minister announced major reductions in federal transfers to the provinces for social programs, indicating that the need to reduce the federal fiscal deficit was a higher priority. Within 2 years and before the entire program of spending reductions had been implemented, the government was projecting a surplus budget in the near future.

In sum, since 1980 governments have attempted to restrain social-program spending on almost all fronts. Some of their efforts have been successful; others have not. Attempts to reduce costs have in some areas been offset by cost increases in others. Until the early 1990s, the reductions tended to be phased in gradually. However, the measures introduced in recent years have been more dramatic, including federal reductions in transfers to provinces and provincial actions to reduce social-assistance benefits and restructure health care. In 1996, the federal government replaced the Canada Assistance Plan with the Canada Health and Social Transfer, which altered federal–provincial finance formulas for health, education, and social-security programs. These changes profoundly affected the sustainability of national standards relating to the social safety net and entailed serious spending cutbacks. The impact of these changes has not yet been evaluated nationally, although net overall spending reductions are beginning to be more apparent. Evidence of social stress is being reported in the form of increased levels of poverty among vulnerable groups, increased homelessness, and increased concerns about personal safety (Schellenberg and Ross 1997).

Do these changes constitute a paradigm shift? Does it mean that a whole new theoretical base for social policy has been developed? As yet, it seems not. Most changes have been introduced to reduce government spending, with mixed levels of success. However, the waves of change and adaptation are accumulating, and it is important to consolidate the lessons and insights that come out of the reform process, with a view to preparing for a new model to evolve.

Conclusions and implications of reform

An overall assessment

Over the second half of the century, social conditions in Canada have generally been on an improving trajectory. Poverty rates, whether measured on an absolute or a relative scale, have been declining, although they have declined much more slowly in the past two decades. Overall population poverty in Canada decreased from 16.8% in 1971 to 11.7% in 1991 (according to the UNDP scale; UNDP 1997). However, this positive measure tends to mask some important negative developments, including an increase in wage and income polarization and an increasing reliance among lower income groups on government transfer programs. Between 1984 and 1994, the incidence of "market poverty" among working-age families (defined as the percentage of families below the low-income line *before* the application of government transfers) remained constant at 22.8%. This figure disguises the fact that these poverty rates improved by up to 2% for families with a family head between the ages of 45 and 64, but the poverty rates regressed by as much as 13% for younger working families (Schellenberg and Ross 1997).

Although real individual earnings dropped sharply in many cases (and rose sharply in a few others), average family incomes did not change much. Despite the economic changes, stability was sustained in broad patterns of family-income inequality during the 1980s and early 1990s. Falling real wages were offset by a combination of greater female participation in the formal labour market; mature pension plans, which sustained incomes of displaced unionized workers; and increasing government expenditures on income-support programs. Also, some delay occurred in the formation of new low-income families as underemployed young adults remained economically dependent on their parents.

Despite continuous efforts to reduce government spending on social programs, the proportion of the economy taken up by social spending continued to increase. From 14.9% of GDP in 1966, social spending increased to 21.7% in 1976, and to 23.7% in 1990, and surpassed 28% in 1996 (Hunsley 1992 and StatsCan 1997). Although benefits were reduced in many programs, the overall demand for social security increased throughout the period because of increased unemployment, decreased labour-market revenues among young families, and workers leaving the labour force, either through pension or disability programs (Hunsley 1997b). During this period, government spending also increased as a proportion of GDP (UNDP 1997).

Service reductions were visible in the health-care field, especially in services delivered by hospitals and public institutions. Fees for universities and other programs for post-secondary education significantly increased, doubled in many cases.

In all, to date, social-policy reforms have made most programs less generous and, in some cases, reduced caseloads by decreasing the range of eligibility. As a result of both the accumulated social damage of the economic transformation and an increased population in need of service, the overall costs have not decreased. Most recent indications are that actual social spending has decreased because of a combination of sustained economic growth; low interest rates, reducing the burden of the federal debt on operating budgets; and the accumulated impact of previous spending reductions.

Although the costs have not been reduced, the distribution of those costs is changing. The federal financial role in provincial programs is diminishing. Program users and their families are taking on a larger share of the costs. Program costs are also being pushed from one source to another in a system that is becoming more complex. Because of the combinations of benefits and accessible services, removing candidates from a program may result in as many or more costs turning up elsewhere. For example, reductions in unemployment protection may trigger increases in social-assistance and disability-insurance costs. Alternatively, copayment requirements for the purchase of drugs or user fees for preventive services may dissuade some modest-income people from seeking assistance in a timely manner, with the result that more expensive assistance is required later on for untreated conditions. These risks increase when program benefits are narrowly targeted.

In considering the 1994 Social Security Review, one might conclude that the overriding momentum of the previous political direction, usually typified as neoliberal, supplanted the attempt to gain a new vision for social policy. However, despite the rhetoric about a "new paradigm" and "reinventing" or "rolling back" government, taxation and social spending have both increased; the state accounts for more of the economy than before; and social programs account for an increased portion of both state spending and the economy.

In 1997, economic indicators appear to be still on an upswing. A growing economy may bring opportunities to seek and consolidate a new vision for social policy. As the current processes of change (privatization, downsizing of government operations, decentralization, reduced benefits, increased user fees, etc.) accumulate, they will eventually enable a new configuration of policies and programs to emerge. The rationalization, integration, and consolidation of the new pattern, with the increased complexity of actors, programs, and consumer groups, will constitute the real paradigm shift in social policy. Nonetheless, some important lessons and implications for policy reconceptualization and reformulation are emerging from the overall experience.

Governance issues

The Canadian experience in social-policy reform will be an important factor in the evolution of the federal system. Political leaders and analysts have begun talking about the future shape of the Canadian federation as emerging through an evolution of "the social union." The shape of the new union has not yet emerged, but the outlines are becoming clearer.

When the federal government put into place new financing options in the past, not all provinces would take up the new arrangements right away, and when provinces wanted to change their systems, they had to consider the financial implications carefully if their new policies failed to meet federal conditions. This moderating effect on public-policy changes appears to be decreasing as federal financial participation in provincial programs declines. Provinces can now make more rapid and far-reaching changes because those change have less potential impact on federal transfers.

The provinces will likely be dominant in determining the shape of future social policy. The federal government will have a continuing presence, but there will be a shift in emphasis from financial partnerships with provinces to leadership based on policy exchange, information coordination, experimentation, and the rights and responsibilities of citizenship. A consensus is developing for the federal and provincial governments to share responsibility for the social and economic wellbeing of the population and for there to be cooperation, rather than competition, in pursuit of fiscal and policy objectives. A current initiative to design a combined federal–provincial tax benefit for children may be a prototype for future social security, in that it requires cooperation and accountability, without an actual transfer of funds from one government to another. In this case, the federal government will increase its support for children of low-income working parents and accept a greater proportion of the costs for children of parents on social assistance, on condition that the provinces agree to reinvest their savings in areas affecting low-income children. However, the specific areas of reinvestment are not predetermined, and this leaves the provinces broad scope in meeting their responsibilities.

It is also likely that local government will have an increased role in social policy, especially when governments implement decentralization policies and more diverse delivery systems. The need for effective integration of policy, delivery, and local political accountability will increase as the mix of both federal and provincial and public and private policies and delivery systems becomes more complex.

Public consultation versus federal–provincial negotiations

Federal and provincial governments usually initiate a consultation process before introducing major changes. This allows stakeholders to come forward with their concerns or suggestions. Often their case is for clear standards and government accountability for the quality of programs, conditions of access, and other factors of public interest. Inevitably, not all of the participants are pleased with the results. Nonetheless, the process does permit people to be heard.

However, many federal and provincial government decisions involve the calculation, negotiation, and transfer of money. The clearest standards and accountability are usually found in the definition of financial arrangements. Yet, the financial discussions take place out of public view; the financial terminology is complex; and the documents are not well circulated. As a result, frustration is felt by the public, who feel excluded from the process, and by officials, who feel that the public does not understand the complexities of policy issues. The process of social-policy reform highlights the need to bring clearer public accountability to the interface between governments while giving each government enough flexibility to exercise its own mandate.

Rebuilding amid fragmentation and complexity

As explained earlier, the Canadian social-policy structure evolved incrementally, with the gradual accumulation of a complex array of policies and programs. Because of this and the particular characteristics of Canadian federal politics, the reform process has been fragmented and inconsistent. The public may perceive current changes as socially deconstructive and confusing, with entitlements gradually being removed and responsibilities for support services or for economic security being off-loaded to lower levels of government, to charitable organizations, or to families. Resulting family stress and increased demands on individuals' time have become broad public concerns. Governments are now required to manage the increased complexity of the system that has followed the shift toward more highly differentiated and targeted programs.

Policy issues are increasingly tackled from a horizontal angle, with coordinated policy action required across a range of departments, institutions, and levels of government. Many policy objectives cannot be achieved through the actions of government alone and require the orchestration of public, private, community, and family resources. A major challenge to future social policy will be to find an appropriate and socially just balance among these participants. A new policy-deliberation structure that incorporates government fiscal concerns in a cooperative framework and includes NGOs and commercial and institutional interests as partners in the process will need to evolve.

Although public policy will influence the broad sweep of individual and community life, the orchestration of resources will make results more difficult to measure in relation to the output of specific programs. Better measures of social-policy outcomes will be needed to incorporate the broader range of actors and factors. Service-delivery systems will need to respond to increased complexity with fewer resources.

Some of the new directions will be as follows:

- Decentralized structures will be established for service delivery.

- New systems will be established for coordination of access and resource allocation among a widening array of competing service agencies, professions, and private service providers. These include "gateway services," which ensure that individuals are referred only to needed services; and "diversion services," which attempt to divert people into less expensive service streams. Examples include community-service options or negotiated restitution rather than the courts and prisons for offenders; and home- or community-based services rather than institutions for dependent elderly people or people with major disabilities.

- New client–server technology will be introduced to permit the integration of client files from a variety of different programs. This has potential for dramatic savings in the management of services, especially across programs with similar processes of application for benefits, adjudication of eligibility, verification of information, and service-eligibility reminders. Many government programs are actively adopting the technology to increase the efficiency of their own operations. In the near future, however, one can expect that several different programs, even from different jurisdictions, will be rolled into common delivery systems.

Research issues

Social outcomes

The reform process has focused closer attention on the outcomes of programs and policy. The focus is on achieving results, especially as many of the efforts to reduce costs have failed. Concerns are also being raised about the credibility of those indicators that suggest the economy is healthy and growing while people feel that important dimensions of the quality of life are diminishing. Several organizations, including the Federation of Canadian Municipalities, are putting new social-monitoring systems in place. They are emphasizing the need to measure policy outcomes in relation to the social conditions of the population (social outcomes), rather than measuring outputs of specific programs, when assessing social-policy reforms.

Social-outcome measurement to assess government performance is in part easy and in part difficult. It is both intuitively appropriate to the community and relatively easy to measure the social conditions of the population. However, these conditions reflect the integrated results of several factors — public policies, economic conditions, and private actions — and it is not so easy to determine which portion of any particular outcome is attributable to public policy. An example of a methodological improvement in this area is a recent trend toward measuring market poverty and poverty after government taxes and transfers to more clearly determine the effect of public policy. More research in this area will undoubtedly lead to similar refinements in other outcome measures.

Global and domestic drivers of reform

Social policies and programs are being reformed in many countries and regions. National governments are reacting to strong economic forces, social and demographic pressures, and evolving political realities. They are elaborating new policy objectives and new policy structures within more globally integrated cultural, fiscal, and institutional frameworks.

Many social-policy concerns are more clearly becoming international, such as the international portability of social-security entitlements. International agreements and reciprocal legislative provisions now link the social-security systems of several countries, with individual pension entitlements calculated and delivered by one country on behalf of another. Canada has negotiated reciprocal arrangements with many other countries. Population movement and the needs of immigrants and refugees constitute another transnational concern. Countries on both the receiving and the sending sides of the exchange need to cooperate in the regulation of the flow of people and labour.

Population-health concerns are also being tackled on an increasingly transnational basis.

The new technology of program-delivery systems and its provision and management by the private sector are leading to increased potential for the compatibility of systems. This means that large private organizations, such as banks and international consulting or accounting firms, may be able to offer their services to various countries to supplement or replace existing public structures. Globalization is not limited to commercial transactions. Communications, culture, and processes of governance are also caught up in the wave of change. What then of social policy? Could the processes of social-policy reform at national levels lead to the international and transnational integration of important dimensions of social policy? Might we witness the development of regional and global social-policy structures? More focused research is needed on the international dimensions of social policy, the shared experiences, and the evolution of shared policy-development frameworks and processes.

However, social policy still encompasses overwhelmingly domestic preoccupations, as it deals primarily with national residents; with the benefits and responsibilities of citizenship; and with collective national resources. Social policy is becoming increasingly important as the central instrument of the nation-state to promote social solidarity. The health, well-being, and adaptability of the population and the social policy that tackles these concerns can constitute the "social glue" of the nation-state. Moreover, country-specific situations can vary significantly. The demographic profiles of countries, even of those in the same region, can be quite different. The health status of the population and the educational profiles can vary. Religion and culture can play a dominant or weak role in the formulation of policy. The mix of domestic social problems — poverty, ill health, training needs, crime — require country-specific responses with unique dimensions.

The Canadian experience indicates that economic globalization has provided both strong pressure and a powerful political-economic context for social-policy reform. One of the strongest factors has been increased sensitivity to the response of international financial markets among those responsible for the formulation of domestic fiscal policy. During the 1980s, Canada's national debt was transformed from a primarily domestic one to a primarily foreign one, and the concerns of investors and currency traders resonated in the pronouncements of federal politicians. And yet, it is important to note that Canadian social policy still differs significantly from that of the United States and that, in Canada, reductions have not been as dramatic as those in the United Kingdom or New Zealand. In fact, the social-policy record of OECD countries in the 1980s reveals that these countries made distinct policy choices, even when they were faced with similar international forces. In more recent years, the patterns in once diverse countries appear to be converging. This is similar to a storm at sea, when ships with different destinations are blown in the same direction.

Transcending conceptual and information boundaries

A major challenge for future social-policy research with an international dimension is to find the means to transcend the traditional boundaries between OECD countries and the developing world. A conceptual and methodological divide between these worlds has sometimes seemed to hinder the formulation of policy research.

This is not to suggest that no change is evident. National policy frameworks are becoming more comparable. Issues such as decentralization, the integration of policy, accountability at local levels, and the role of civil society in policy development and implementation are of common concern. The Internet is providing major new possibilities for researchers around the globe to share their analyses and to access similar data. Even the transnationalism of private enterprises that are providing public services opens new doors to international policy research.

The terminology of research will likely become more consistent over time, and the measurements will likely become more consistent across national boundaries. Consequently, one can envision that a unifying factor for research will be a transnational focus on the measurement of socioeconomic outcomes for quality of life. The HDI of the UNDP is already having such an effect in many countries. More indepth measures will undoubtedly evolve.

Another area for potential cross-national sharing, which is not too constrained by the need for consistent statistical data, is in recent best-practices research. Although *best* may be a debatable label for many practices, the focus is really on sharing the knowledge of new developments. This is essential because traditional research and dissemination methods are slow. The challenge will be to develop the best filtering and assessment techniques to ensure that research is accurate and appropriate, with unbiased analysis and interpretation.

Chapter 5

Conclusion

A Research Agenda for Social-policy Reform

Jennifer L. Moher[1]

In the 1990s, social-policy reform has emerged as a critical area for development-policy research. A number of trends have led policymakers to reconsider social safety nets in both the North and the South. Globalization, human mobility, communications, trade, and capital flows have combined with fiscal conservatism and structural-adjustment strategies to fundamentally alter both the principles and the practice of social policy in key sectors. As the case studies on Ghana, Chile, and Canada in this volume have highlighted, decentralization, privatization, cost-sharing, and targeting measures are just some of the recent reforms affecting the ways social services are designed, financed, implemented, and delivered.

Recognition of the changing nature and importance of social policy is reflected in the recent emergence at the international level of a distinct discourse on social development. In the developing world, toward the end of the 1980s, mounting concern with the social impact of structural-adjustment policies culminated in 1990 with the publication of the United Nations Development Programme's first *Human*

---

[1] Jennifer Moher is a Research Associate with the Assessment of Social Policy Reforms program initiative at the International Development Research Centre, Canada.

Development Report, which focused explicitly on the plight of the world's poorest people. A similar dynamic has emerged in the North, with the crisis of the welfare state. Growing pressure to revisit social issues has surfaced in the developed world in the 1990s as the governments of countries in the Organisation for Economic Co-operation and Development (OECD) have had to struggle with the challenges of competitiveness, persistent unemployment, and deficit management, together with growing public concern about the social costs of conservative socioeconomic reforms.

These changes have in the North and the South contributed to a significant shift in development thinking. Beginning in the early years of this decade and in large part driven by the backlash against narrowly defined economic reforms and perspectives, strong support has emerged for a more balanced approach to development, one that integrates both social and economic objectives without subordinating the one to the other. Opposition to the priority given to economic concerns has led to a renewed emphasis on social development, reflected in global conferences such as the 1990 Summit for Children, the 1990 Education Conference for All, the 1994 Cairo Conference on Population, the 1995 Beijing Conference on Women, and the 1995 Copenhagen Summit for Social Development. Moreover, as the 1997 *Human Development Report* made clear, some very sobering realities justify this renewed concern with social development. Following nearly two decades of adjustment, sub-Saharan Africa is currently home to 220 million people who suffer from income poverty, and the human poverty level is growing faster there than anywhere else in the world. In Latin America and the Caribbean, structural inequality is pervasive, and the level of income poverty stands at 110 million people and is rising. In the industrialized world, more than 100 million people now live below the income poverty line (UNDP 1997).

If social development now tops the global agenda and if the case studies included here have underlined real interest, in both the North and the South, in finding a socially sustainable approach to reform, important challenges remain concerning the way forward. This concluding chapter suggests that in recent years the development literature has tended to be polarized between the competing perspectives of mainstream neoliberals and their critics. The result is that much development thinking and debate on economic and social policy (and its reform) have tended to be fairly normative. However, as countries try to find ways to address the social implications of neoliberal reforms to date and researchers and practitioners are encouraged by the possibility of a more balanced development strategy, there is a growing need to move beyond criticism of these policies to a more systematic and empirically informed examination of the factors influencing their design, articulation, and impacts. The three case studies in this volume have made an attempt to do this.

This chapter is therefore divided into two main sections. The first provides a brief sketch of the relevant debates in the recent development literature, outlining the different perspectives of the neoliberal school and its critics and the new integrationist alternative. The second section explores in detail some essential elements of a future agenda for research on social-policy reform. It contends that an emerging literature — including these studies of Ghana, Chile, and Canada — underlines that some of the key issues for future research will be found at the level of policy implementation, where the theory of social-policy reform is put into practice.

Neoliberalism, its critics, and the integrationist alternative

Neoliberalism and its critics

Over the past two decades, the development debate has been largely oriented by neoliberal theories and prescriptions for reform. In the developing world, in response to the economic downturn and debt crisis of the 1970s, the International Monetary Fund and the World Bank pressed for structural-adjustment packages premised on the theory and practice of neoliberalism. Core elements of these packages included deregulation of economies, trade liberalization, export promotion, currency devaluation, strengthening of the financial sector, and public-sector reform. Moreover, parallel to these trends, similar changes were under way in the industrialized OECD countries. Recession in the early 1980s, following the preceding oil shock, resulted in high inflation and unemployment, with consequent growth in demands for state assistance. The Keynesian approach to economic management had been discredited, and "confidence in the state's ability to manage a mixed economy" had collapsed (Mishra 1984, p. 190).

Theories therefore emerged from the right that, in addition to rejecting Keynesianism, championed policies to limit the scope of state interventionism and encourage market forces (Pulkingham and Ternowetsky 1998). Privatization, deregulation, promotion of freer trade, and fiscal conservatism have since emerged as dominant forces, with the aim of reconfiguring and, some assert, dismantling welfare states in the North.

As reflected in the case studies in this volume, neoliberal reforms have pervasively and definitively come to inform development strategies, including social policies, in many countries. In the developing world particularly, from Latin America to Africa, many have considered structural adjustment a blueprint for achieving both economic and social goals. It was initially expected that by promoting economic growth, structural-adjustment measures would produce a "trickle down" of benefits to the most vulnerable groups in society. Poverty, according to neoliberal theory, is a pathology, rather than a consequence of the economic system, and should be addressed primarily with measures aimed at economic recovery. Social policies, or state actions aimed at tailoring economic growth to serve explicitly social objectives and needs, have therefore remained implicitly separate and subordinate to overarching economic priorities.

More than just an economic theory, however, neoliberalism is also a political theory. Where neoliberals have called for economic conservatism and the preeminence of the market, they have also supported the theory of a minimal state. Structural adjustment in the South and post-Keynesian reform in the North have curtailed public expenditures, including social expenditures, to achieve deficit and inflation reduction. In addition, public agencies and bureaucracies have been cut back in the interest of efficiency, and state intervention in the economy has been minimized to prevent unwanted distortions and "crowding out" of private-sector investment. With market forces cast as the primary engine of development and the means of attaining social welfare (increasingly individualistic), a concurrent approach to social policy has been broadly perceived as inherently residual, or ex post facto, as suggested throughout this volume.

Not surprisingly, critical appraisals of neoliberal reforms have been extensive and diverse. In the development literature, some critics have challenged the technical premises of the reforms and have engaged in a range of debates concerning the causes of the initial economic crisis and, by consequence, the appropriateness and adequacy of adjustment packages introduced in specific national contexts (for example, see Glover 1991; Sinha 1995). Other critical perspectives on neoliberal reform have been more overtly political or ideological. In both developed and developing countries, some of the most articulate criticism of mainstream reform models has come from the left, which has viewed neoliberal prescriptions and, particularly, the promotion of market-friendly states as favouring the interests of private capital over human well-being and as valuing efficiency and profit over social equity. Challenging neoliberal discourse, which characterizes economies as "self-regulating" and current adjustment strategies as "inevitable," these schools have highlighted the inherently political nature of the reforms and forwarded alternative theoretical perspectives on the state, the market, and the vested interests they each serve (for example, see Brodie 1994; Tsie 1996; Power 1997).

An element common throughout most of this critical literature in both the North and the South is its focus on the social costs of reform and on the dangers associated with the state's decreasing role in development, particularly in social spheres and commitments. In OECD countries, rising poverty levels, jobless growth, and stubborn structural unemployment have produced heightened levels of social need and fueled concern about the costs of government retrenchment, social-spending cuts, diminished labour protection, and trends away from universal, state-supported social policies toward programs perceived as more restrictive, exclusionary, and less generous (for example, see Geller and Joel 1997; Pulkingham and Ternowetsky 1997, 1998). The critical literature in the North has particularly emphasized the implications of welfare-state restructuring, or "erosion," for class- and gender-based political agency and inequality, and significant criticism has focused on the perceived abnegation of state responsibilities for public welfare and basic standards of social equity and access to services (Brodie 1994).

In non-OECD countries, the dismal economic record of structural-adjustment policies and the perception that they have had far-reaching negative social effects have fueled broad-based criticism of these policies. In the developing world, concerns about the social implications of the neoliberal agenda have been expressed through extensive research on the practical burden that economic reforms have placed on grass-roots groups (for example, see Afshar 1992; Jolly et al. 1992; Bakker

1994; Sen 1996). Indeed, central to the critique of structural adjustment in the South has been the evidence, now generally accepted, that neoliberal packages have in fact seriously exacerbated poverty levels and distributional inequalities. Contrary to the early expectation that social development would materialize as a by-product of economic growth, 10–15 years of reform have seen much more dire results. Although debates persist concerning specific causal relationships — in particular, on whether the cause is the economic crisis or adjustment packages — persistent correlations between structural adjustment and social hardship have captured the attention of development analysts. In the 1980s, Africa and Latin America saw real per capital incomes, living standards, and investment levels drop. Today, Latin America has lower standards of living than in the 1970s, and in Africa, levels approximate those of the late 1960s (Karger 1996; Berry 1997).

Reflecting the unifying concern of all these perspectives and the social impact of the neoliberal reform packages, broad-based criticism of structural adjustment was initially and perhaps most prominently captured in the United Nations Children's Fund's call in the late 1980s for adjustment with "a human face." Similar rejections of the market-as-magic-bullet approach to reform have also surfaced in industrialized countries, with growing public support for socially responsible fiscal reform and socially accountable government.

The integrationist alternative

Debates between neoliberals and their critics have constituted the principal poles of the debate in the development literature in recent years. However, the practical implications of this dialogue, particularly from a policy and research perspective, are considered somewhat tenuous in the literature. Whereas critics of the neoliberal school have highlighted real weaknesses of the dominant economic paradigm, others suggest that the strength of the critics' perspective has been in their theoretical and social critique of neoliberalism, rather than in their articulation of a cogent and defensible alternative. Indeed, the predominant focus of this critical literature on the social failings of neoliberal reform has spurred charges that it has merely challenged imperfect mainstream models from the perspective of equally unsustainable interventionist or welfarist strategies that still leave too much in the hands of the state (Glover 1991; Patel 1992; Green 1996).

Scepticism about the contribution of the critics of neoliberalism has also been reinforced by recent historical trends: the dramatic and recent failure of socialist economies has undermined proposed alternatives to a market-oriented approach.

If something of a stalemate has developed along familiar ideological fault lines — that is, neoliberal versus welfarist–socialist approaches to development — a third school seeks to be more forward looking and prescriptive. As Green (1996, p. 118) observed,

> The transformation of the world economy in the last 30 years may have destroyed full-blown central planning as a viable economic model, but [the social toll of structural adjustment means that] crude neoliberal dogma also offers little hope for long-term success ... . Although opponents of structural adjustment are routinely dismissed as economic dinosaurs bereft of alterative ideas, there is already a rich debate over the ingredients for building a more effective economic model.

Referred to by such labels as "post-welfarist," "neostructuralist," or (as here) "integrationist," this alternative model puts emphasis on the need to simultaneously pursue and integrate economic and social-development objectives and strategies. The model is broadly distinguished by several basic tenets. These include the recognition of

- The validity of the adjustment challenge in the developed and developing worlds and the need to respond through economic and social-policy reforms to a range of real pressures arising from globalization, competitiveness, and interdependence;

- The importance of selective and regulative state interventions to counterbalance the effects of the market in the context of reform;

- The need to build synergies, or "partnerships," between the public and private sectors to maximize efficiency and safeguard equity;

- The importance of having responsibilities for social welfare shared between states and societies in the context of limited state capacities and resources and persistent basic needs; and

- The importance of participatory, people-centred development strategies that promote the responsiveness and sustainability of policies by reinforcing democracy.

In short, in the North and in the South, this philosophy tends to be pragmatic concerning economic growth, fiscal responsibility, and economic adjustment but to combine this with a concern for collective welfare, civic responsibility, and the public good.

The integrationist perspective is surfacing more frequently in contributions to international-development literature and discourse. In the academic sphere, for instance, examples of the integrationist perspective can be found in an alternative economic literature that challenges long-standing assumptions about the relationship between economic growth, social investment, and equality. Furthermore, economists are questioning traditional theories premised on a contradictory relationship between economic growth and equality, which have generally viewed public social investment as an obstacle to growth. Revisionist analyses now argue that neither of these connections is inevitable and that far from being a drain on growth, public social expenditures in such areas as health, housing, and education may in fact enhance productivity and economic performance. This recent literature stresses that state and policy play a potentially critical role in facilitating growth with equity, and in support of this contention many analysts are pointing to the impressive economic- and social-development track records of the Asian newly industrialized countries (NICs) (Amsden 1989; Wade 1990; Sherraden 1995; Kelly 1997; McKay 1997).

Similar arguments also more popularly appear in current international-development forums and discourse. Thus, the final report of the World Conference on Social Development (United Nations 1995, p. 13) emphasized the need to

> promote dynamic, open, free markets, while recognizing the need to intervene in markets to the extent necessary to prevent or counteract market failure, promote stability and longterm investment ... and harmonize economic and social development.

Summit resolutions called for an "integrated approach to the transformation process, addressing the social consequences of reforms and human development needs" (United Nations 1995, p. 32). Moreover, echoing the views of a growing range of international bodies, including the United Nations Research Institute for Social Development (UNRISD) and the Economic Commission for Latin America and the Caribbean, similar prescriptions surfaced in the 1997 *Human Development Report*, which emphasized the importance of "pro-poor economic growth," "people centred strategies," and an "activist," or "managerial," state, capable of engineering both economic growth and poverty eradication. Indeed, as development discourse increasingly problematizes social goals, as distinct from economic ones, some have observed that even the international financial institutions (IFIs) are "stealing the clothes" of the integrationist school by placing renewed emphasis on concepts such as education, poverty alleviation, and income redistribution, albeit within the context of market-oriented reform (WCSD 1995; Green 1996).

If the integrationist school proposes an alternative set of possibilities and objectives for socially responsive growth, it is not without its own detractors. Integrationism is considered by some to be a broad church, with weak analytic or policy content and prescriptions (Green 1996). However, it should also be recognized that, far from constituting a new theme, debates over the appropriate balance between the state and market in achieving development goals have in fact constituted a consistent thread in the development literature. For example, before the 1990s, the recommendation that development strategies should reflect a tempered approach, based on both social and economic objectives and values, was evident in a range of international documents: the 1979 United Nations International Development Strategy, the Brandt Report (of 1980), and the United Nations Declaration on the Right to Development (of 1986), to name but a few (Patel 1992).

From the perspective of those who are concerned with future development-policy research, the perennial nature of these reflections and the return of practitioners and scholars in the 1990s to the recognition of the value of mixed formulas suggest three general conclusions. First, the general ideological polarization of the development literature between neoliberalism and its critics may not be particularly useful or productive. It is now generally acknowledged that neither strict market nor state-dominated approaches to development are sustainable options and that continuing to invoke these as reference points in the development debate may obscure more than illuminate. Second, some combination of state, market, and civil-society efforts, together with some integration of social and economic policies, will likely be needed to enable development strategies to achieve their desired social and economic outcomes in real historical contexts. To acknowledge this, however, is still to leave a great many questions unanswered about the sustainable and optimal linkages and divisions of responsibility between the actors and the factors that condition their roles in specific policy contexts. Third, and as a consequence, some of the most important questions for policy-planning and policy-development research are likely to lie at the operational level. In short, if a perspective on general principles for a more balanced development paradigm is emerging (a new model for social protection based on articulated social and economic policies and strengthened sociopolitical integration, as Raczynski suggests in this volume), a constructive approach to social and economic policies will have to move beyond normative debates and criticism of these policies to a more contextually informed analysis of how these policies are implemented in practice and why they take the forms they do.

The next section returns to the more specific focus of this book, the assessment of social-policy reform in the developing and developed worlds. Drawing selectively on the case studies, as well as on a wider literature, it considers some of the major changes in the nature and orientation of social policies in the 1990s. It suggests that the most important issues for research, particularly from the perspective of promoting a more economically and socially sustainable approach to development, are likely to involve empirical research on the design and implementation of recent reforms and on the political, social, and institutional contexts that shape their success or failure. The discussion is organized around four general themes: the decentralization, privatization, targeting, and democratization of social policies. They are common to all three of the case studies and are currently at the heart of policy agendas and public debate in the North and South.

Social-policy reform: exploring issues for research

Decentralization of social policy

Central to social-policy reform in the developed and developing world has been the sweeping trend to decentralize social policy. As the studies in this volume illustrate, movement away from state- or welfare-oriented models has been matched in the 1980s and 1990s by significant initiatives to redistribute responsibilities for social policy and social-service delivery to subnational actors, particularly local governments, nongovernmental organizations (NGOs), and communities. Decentralization is occurring in the context of broader debates concerning sustainable and appropriate roles for the state versus other actors in social and economic development. From the neoliberal perspective, prescriptions for a noninterventionist state are closely tied to the devolution of authority and responsibility for social policy and services to local levels. Preoccupied with promoting "good governance," these advocates point to the expected windfalls of decentralization in terms of the efficiency, effectiveness, and responsiveness of social programs as designed and delivered by (smaller) organizations closer to the grass roots (Vilas 1996; Stewart 1997). Neoliberals are not the only proponents of decentralization, however. In the 1980s and 1990s, an intellectual movement has emphasized development as empowerment, the need to go beyond the state and market to the community, and popular participation as the goal, means, and agency of development (Veltmeyer 1997). Thus, quite apart from its expected impacts on efficiency and costs, decentralization has also been viewed as a means to improve community-based involvement and enhance political accountability and democracy, issues of central concern to critics of the mainstream reform agenda.

Notwithstanding this wide support, however, a growing body of work, including the case studies in this volume, suggests that the potential of decentralization as an approach to the design, delivery, and financing of social services can be assessed most reliably through a greater understanding of those factors that motivate and affect the practical articulation of these reforms. What seems to be required is critical consideration of the fundamental assumptions underpinning decentralization strategies as measured against the conditions for, and experience of, their implementation.

An issue emphasized throughout this volume is the important and evolving role of NGOs in the field of social policy. In the context of recent economic- and social-policy reform, the number, budgets, and influence of NGOs in both the North and the South have increased remarkably. Some promote the role of NGOs as the new "miracle weapon" in the fight against poverty, and much greater levels of foreign aid are now transferred through the NGOs, rather than through public agencies (Post and Preuss 1997). Where concerns predominate about the capacity and effectiveness of states in the North and South, the expectation is widespread that NGOs will become a feasible alternative to state agencies as agents of development. This faith in NGOs is largely based on the assumption that NGOs tend by nature to be more participatory, innovative, unbureaucratic, flexible, and inclusive than state structures (UNRISD 1995; Smillie 1997; Stewart 1997).

NGOs are far from constituting a magic solution, however, as important questions are beginning to be raised about the real nature and capacities of NGOs as measured against the roles and responsibilities given to them. Most generally, development analysts are increasingly warning that the advantages of NGOs can be overestimated, not because of what NGOs are, but because of what they are not, that is, the state. The assumption is too readily made that if states are deemed inefficient, elitist, and unresponsive, anything else — in particular, NGOs — must be better (Clark 1992). Assertions of this type are too often made without the support of empirical analysis. Moreover, this type of negative reasoning is too often compounded by tendencies to confuse the state with particular types of regime. As a result, especially in the developing world, state capacities or potential — whatever these might be — are mistakenly conflated and rejected along with authoritarian government (Allen 1997).

More central to the literature and studies presented here, however, are the critical assessments of the NGOs' institutional capacity to substitute for the state in welfare protection and social-service provision. For example, Post and Preuss (1997) pointed out that little real evidence supports the view that NGOs are more effective or efficient than alternative state agencies, and they may in fact be limited, rather than advantaged, by their size, capacity, and core missions. Post and Preuss argued that NGOs tend to be diverse, to focus on discrete rather than broad-reaching interventions or projects, and to work uncoordinatedly. This lack of harmonization, moreover, may be compounded by patterns of finance. As Stewart (1997) suggested, public-sector services can take the long view and thus risk fewer gaps, overlaps, and contradictions in their programing, whereas NGOs, because of their number and their short-term funding, possess less capacity for innovation and have a greater tendency to be repetitive in practice. Problems in coordination and in maintaining coherent social interventions are also exacerbated by the tendency of NGOs to scale up in response to enhanced responsibilities and availability of funds: if NGOs possess inherently positive qualities associated with their small size and proximity to the constituencies they serve, these very qualities are undermined by the NGOs' own tendency to become larger, more bureaucratic, and less accountable when the state retreats and the state and the donors place greater weight on the NGOs' ability to deliver (Howes and Sattar 1992; Stewart 1997). Such risks seem to be borne out in the Ghanaian experience reported in this volume. As Aryeetey and Goldstein detail, the decentralization of responsibility for social policy to NGOs under the Economic Recovery Program and structural-adjustment plan in Ghana faltered precisely as a result of such factors as the uneven geographical distribution of NGOs, their small scale and diverse mandates, and their constrained ability to undertake coordinated activities. Moreover, echoing similar concerns in the literature, Aryeetey and Goldstein also suggest that as NGOs and donors increasingly collaborate to deliver social services the unfortunate unintended effect may be to weaken the capacity and commitment of states and NGOs to undertake the activities they are respectively best suited to provide.

A third set of critical issues for research on decentralization relates to process and implementation. As emphasized throughout this book, in both the North and the South, the motive and context for decentralization has largely been the perceived requisites of economic adjustment and deficit management. Rather than representing a rationalized or strategic approach to improving the management and delivery of social services, the decentralization of social policy from central levels to local government, NGOs, and communities has often been the result of public-expenditure cutbacks and resource constraints. With reference to Latin America, Vilas (1996, p. 24) summarized the problem as follows:

> Up to now, decentralization ... has focussed on programme implementation, not program design. This amounts to functional decentralization, also referred to as "deconcentration" — but not political decentralization ... . Virtually overnight, for example, municipalities have found themselves responsible for providing a gamut of social services without the necessary financial, human, administrative and material resources. This often translates into inefficiency ... in service delivery, deterioration in the quality of services, and the emergence of multiple entities that perform functions that used to be the responsibility of a single institution.

Such obstacles to effective decentralization have resonance beyond Latin America and are reflected in all three studies in this volume. A number of factors have hampered regionalization and municipalization initiatives in Chile and the sectoral-decentralization efforts under the National Development Planning Commission in Ghana. These factors include insufficient redistribution of authority and decision-making powers; ambiguous guidelines for reorganization and revised mandates; limited local capacities, human resources, and appropriate expertise; inadequate transfer of financial resources; and limited local capacities for revenue generation. In Canada, moreover, challenges have been similar. According to Hunsley, the decentralization of social policy and, particularly, the revised mechanisms for financing it have served to weaken national standards and federal influence over provincial programs. In addition, the devolution to provinces, municipalities, and communities of greater responsibilities, if not greater resources and institutional support, for social-service financing and delivery has placed the sustainability of the reform process into question. As in Ghana and Chile, in Canada decentralization appears not to have resulted in clear gains in cost, efficiency, or quality; rather, the tendency has been for it to redistribute costs within the system as a whole and fragment and deplete the available services. As both Hunsley and Raczynski suggest, this outcome underscores the importance of evaluation methods and indicators — currently lacking — to capture the real and sometimes obscured costs and benefits of such reforms.

To summarize, then, from the country studies, the appropriateness, benefits, and outcomes of decentralization are neither self-evident nor generalizable across contexts. In some cases, the state's retention of some essential commitments and functions may actually be more feasible and desirable than a diffused approach. Also, development-policy researchers and practitioners who seek better and more sustainable divisions of labour between the state and local entities should pay closer attention to the fundamental assumptions guiding decentralization reforms and the political, social, and institutional factors that influence them. More specifically, the record on decentralization thus far suggests that a future approach will require a focus on such issues as rational and coherent decentralization planning and implementation; strategic institutional-capacity assessment and capacity-building at local-government and nongovernment levels; human-resource training; comprehensive cost–benefit-evaluation frameworks that address the social and economic aspects of the process; and new mechanisms to facilitate policy formulation, accountability, and service delivery in systems that comprise a growing number of actors.

Privatization of social policy

Privatization is another major focus in social-policy reform in the 1990s and is again a recurrent theme throughout this volume. Although privatization is a complex trend that may take several forms, ranging from selective deregulation and subcontracting to wholesale state disinvestiture, it is in general "the transfer of public sector activities to the private sector" (Nyong 1994). As with decentralization, privatization is currently unfolding in the context of wider debates on the appropriate role of the state in development and has been considered a key aspect of the mainstream agenda for economic adjustment. Consistent with commitments to downsize the state, achieve improved allocative efficiency, and alleviate fiscal crises, neoliberals have recommended the sale of state-owned enterprises (SOEs) and the privatization of social-service provision. Moreover, these prescriptions for reform have been embedded in a discourse in which business principles — for example, competitiveness, profit maximization, cost cutting, and individual, or "client," choice — displace traditional public-sector issues and performance yardsticks (Maxwell 1996; Dowbor 1998). Advocates of the privatization paradigm view the state as relatively passive and regulatory, the market as the main and optimal agent of development, and citizens as "consumers" of social services.

Opposition to the privatization of social policy and services has been quite pronounced, however, particularly from the detractors of structural adjustment. Much of the focus has been on the implications of privatization for the poor. As UNRISD (1995, p. 43) observed,

> Neoliberal theory assumes that the market will produce the most efficient and equitable results; assumes that everyone has access to information; and underplays the role of social organization and institutions in shaping economic outcomes and the balance of power between winners and losers.

However, the empirical findings, including those in Aryeetey and Goldstein's study of the Ghanaian case, suggest that the capacity of different groups to benefit from privatization and other reform measures depends in large part on their prereform socioeconomic status. In other words, the concern among critics is that the marketization of public goods previously provided for free may exacerbate existing patterns of inequality. This perspective is grounded more generally in a view that notions of profitability constitute inappropriate criteria for judging the performance of the public sector, which has important responsibilities to public welfare that supersede other goals.

Controversy is more pronounced over the privatization of social services than over their decentralization, largely because the latter is perceived as comprising technical changes in the administration of social policy, rather than changes in the fundamental principles governing provision and entitlement (that is, state provided versus market based). Still, as in the case of decentralization, the recognition is emerging that the conditions for implementation and approaches taken to it can importantly influence the potential for privatization to render social policies more socially and economically sustainable.

The literature on privatization, including the case studies in this volume, suggests some important issues for future investigation. Most prominently, where social-development objectives are a central and growing concern for governments undertaking reform, an obvious research topic is the impact of privatization on vulnerable or disadvantaged groups. As the studies of education- and health-sector reforms in Ghana and Chile in this volume clearly demonstrate, the privatization of services often tends to work to the disadvantage of vulnerable groups by polarizing access and quality of available services between the rich and poor, men and women, and rural and urban groups. Dual and inequitable systems of social-service provision have resulted from reforms that failed to address the impacts of the privatization of services on institutionalized systems of privilege and patterns of resource distribution and allocation. The introduction of fees for services, or user charges — measures that also commercialize or marketize services — has also had effects on these systems and patterns.

The correlation between privatization and inequality justifies specific research and policy attention but also underscores a more general requirement highlighted in the literature: the need for comparative case-study research on the relative benefits and costs of public versus private service provision (Glover 1991). As Cook and Kirkpatrick argued (1997) in their review of the World Bank's *Bureaucrats in Business Report*, no particular reason or empirical evidence suggests that private-sector alternatives are free from the constraints that hinder public-sector performance. Reflecting on the possibility that privatization may or may not produce greater savings and efficiency, Cook and Kirkpatrick (1997, p. 845) contended that

> The Washington consensus [on privatization] ... is a view that is based on some interesting, stimulating, but essentially speculative academic work — work that suggests possibilities, but by no means proves or even makes a compelling empirical case that those possible stories are the right ones.

Although Cook and Kirkpatrick's observations relate principally to the privatization of SOEs, they also have relevance to public social services. For example, MacKintosh (1995) argued that the benefits and risks of privatized social-service provision are context specific. Basing her findings on a review of the literature on health-care provision in the South, MacKintosh underscored that the empirical record on both public and private performance is varied. Arguing that the specific models of public–private partnership in place influence development implications and social outcomes, she and others have pointed to a range of factors as important determinants of social and economic outcomes, including the sequencing of reforms, structure of financing arrangements, power and political leverage of the private sector, and degree of detachment or linkage between public and private components of the system (MacKintosh 1995). Raczynski's review of privatization trends in Chile appears to validate this analysis. On the one hand, the partial privatization of some aspects of health and education services (that is, the provision of nonmedical services within the health sector and the administration of vocational schools) met with some success. Similarly, the privatization of Chile's social-security system may promise some improvement over the previous pay-as-you-go system, although this may be contingent on the ability of the state to encourage stable economic growth and to assert some essential control over such issues as coverage, investment, and access. Conversely and more negatively, a powerful medical lobby has significantly shaped health-care reforms in Chile, with the result that the system now has competition between the sectors for professional resources and links between the two sectors are on balance "detrimental to the former [public sector] and are socially regressive" (Raczynski, this volume, p. 63).

If the benefits and costs of privatization are contingent, a further influential factor concerns the transition from public to privatized provision. In this regard, MacKintosh (1995) pointed out that a major determinant of the social-policy outcomes of privatization is the economic behaviour of public-interest providers, which she argued had been poorly modeled and poorly understood. MacIntosh defined the public-interest sector as including state agencies, NGOs, and commercial providers contracted by the state. The essential argument is that dominant reform models seek to combine centralized social policy-making with a system of service provision that is competitive and diverse in ownership and motivation. The weakness of this approach is its failure to adequately distinguish and anticipate the behaviour of the new public-interest providers. Thus, where states subcontract or devolve responsibility for social-service provision to NGOs, for example, the diversity and nature of these as "nonprofit maximizers" make it difficult to assume that they will demonstrate firm-like or predictable behaviour. Governments not only expect efficiency and cost-saving windfalls in the absence of reliable incentive structures to generate them but more broadly assume the existence of frameworks for coordination and competition between NGOs as public-service providers, rather than verifying or encouraging them. Where broad trends toward NGO-based provision of social services are evident in either the North or the South — as illustrated in the cases studies on Ghana, Chile, and Canada — issues of institutional behaviour and incentive structures have broad relevance across regions and warrant research and policy attention.

Finally, although MacKintosh's analysis focused largely on the subcontracting of services to the nonprofit sector, similar concerns relate to the private sector and commercial providers. Among the most prominent research issues relates to partnerships between the state and the private sector. Analysts — particularly those concerned with social-development goals — point out that the extent to which the criteria of equity and accountability can be ensured under privatization largely depends on the regulatory capacity of the state. In practice, however, this capacity may not be strong or well developed. In Latin America, for example, some note that the state has abdicated or failed to adequately perform this role, with the result being imperfect markets vulnerable to special interests and a risk of oligopolies in sectors such as health, education, or social security (Vilas 1996). As Raczynski observed, moreover, difficult transitions to privatized service may be compounded by such factors as clashes between public and private corporate cultures and — consistent with Aryeetey and Goldstein's findings in Ghana — by the state's giving insufficient attention to the need to attract private-sector interest and investment. Further concerns relate to the actual capacity of the private sector to function as a feasible partner to the state. With reference to Africa, Karger (1996, p. 13) contended that

> The current debate around the privatization of social services has only limited relevance ... . Specifically, this debate assumes the a priori existence of a ready and mature private welfare sector capable of relieving some of the welfare burden from government. However, the existence of a strong for-profit privatized social service sector depends on a well capitalized economic sector that is aggressively searching out new investment opportunities. Furthermore, a for profit sector usually occurs in nations where the social welfare system is underwritten by a longstanding public commitment to providing social services. These conditions are absent in most of Africa.

In sum, the articulation of socially and economically sustainable partnerships between the public and private sectors for the provision of social services appears to depend on a range of factors constructively explored at the implementation, or practical, level.

A priority issue highlighted in this volume, as well as in the wider literature, is the need to understand and address the elements that condition the impact of privatization on social equity. In some cases, a strong state role, rather than a minimalist one, in service provision may be critical because of factors such as the essential nature of the services at issue; the character, level, and distribution of poverty and social needs; and the degree of development of the market. Some important issues present themselves for study if future development trends are to build on the as yet undefined synergies between the public and private sectors, with a bias to exploring further the potential advantages of the market. Specifically, development-policy research will need to address, comparatively and in different national contexts, the relative advantages and disadvantages of different types and degrees of service privatization; the capacities of both public and private institutions and the incentives that govern them in service management and provision; the strengths and dynamism of the relevant markets; the mutual impact of public and private service systems on each other; and the determinants and strengths of the regulatory relationships and mechanisms of accountability between sectors.

Targeting of social policy

The targeting of social policies constitutes a third major element of current social-policy reforms in both the North and the South. The concept is generally understood in two senses: first, in the sense of a technical method of allocating resources strategically within sectors (for example, preventive versus curative health care, primary versus tertiary education); and, second, in the sense of the creation of specific programs or interventions directed at particular groups (for example, poverty-alleviation programs, income-support programs).

As with other aspects of social-policy reform, targeting has stimulated controversy in the literature. Depending on the national-policy context, neoliberals, particularly in the North, have viewed targeting as an appropriate alternative to universal programs, which they deem inefficient and unaffordable in times of fiscal constraint. In the developing world, this perspective is complemented by the view that targeting is an intermediary approach to poverty alleviation that concentrates resources on vulnerable populations during difficult, but transitional, phases of adjustment. By contrast, the critics of the neoliberal approach have argued that targeting represents a wholly insufficient response to poverty. Critics consider temporary or selective responses inadequate in the context of structural adjustment, in which very little evidence indicates any trickling down of benefits. More importantly, critics contend, the targeting of social policies and interventions does little for structurally disadvantaged peoples. As one author asked (Vilas 1996, p. 24) with regard to Latin America, "What does targeting mean when 60–80% of the population is poor?" These detractors tend to altogether discard analyses of the potential and the limits of targeting in favour of reformulating the basic concepts and strategies underpinning the dominant reform agenda.

Where targeting practices have — like other types of reform — been the focus of critical debate on the left and the right, these discussions are nevertheless unfolding in the context of the inevitable requirement of governments in both the North and the South to allocate finite resources in response to persistent and growing human needs. As the cases presented in this volume emphasize, finding a sustainable and effective approach to the allocation and management of social-sector resources stands out as a common preoccupation and commitment of countries across regions. It is again instructive that the literature on targeting underscores a range of factors that may influence, for better or worse, the social and economic impacts of such strategies.

An important set of questions relates to the identification of optimal models for financing targeted programs. In a critical review of antipoverty programs in Latin America, for example, Stahl (1996) focused attention on the Social Investment Funds (SIFs), considered a key aspect of the IFIs' approach to social policy in the region. SIFs are generally externally funded programs aimed at alleviating the social costs of adjustment among the poorest groups. However, as Stahl's analysis suggests, SIFs' record is mixed. Being externally funded, SIFs tend to be vulnerable to funding cuts, tend to discourage domestic commitments to social welfare, and tend to encourage short- rather than long-term perspectives on social issues and social-sector planning. Stahl pointed out that an exception to this characterization was Fondo de Solidaridad e Inversión Social (FOSIS, social solidarity and investment fund), the SIF in Chile. FOSIS differs from other SIFs in the region in that it was established as a permanent feature of state social policy; it is integrated within, rather than isolated from, wider government antipoverty programs; and it places emphasis on long-term capacity- and employment-building projects, rather than on short-term or emergency interventions (Stahl 1996). Stahl's conclusions about SIFs echo Aryeetey and Goldstein's observations concerning the problematic role of foreign funding trends in the social sectors in Ghana. In general, if donor-funded, targeted programs serve to undermine or replace indigenous social-sector spending, the implications for social development may be negative.

Variations in the design and implementation of targeting strategies represent still another important area for investigation. Most generally, it is acknowledged that the success of targeting programs depends on the basic amount of funds available against the size of the population in need, together with the nature and scope of the intervention these funds are used to support. For example, UNRISD indicated that programs aimed at providing social infrastructure, such as schools or clinics, may spread benefits much more widely than more narrowly directed employment-creation schemes (UNRISD 1995).

A third issue that receives considerable attention in this volume is the technical prerequisites and capacities that inform effective targeting strategies. As both the Ghanaian and the Chilean case studies illustrate, if targeted social policies are considered integral to current national development plans — particularly in the context of limited state resources and economic reform — a range of factors, largely associated with technical capacity and infrastructure, may hinder their implementation. As the authors of these case studies stress, public-sector agencies, particularly in the developing world, frequently have underdeveloped information systems; inadequately trained human resources; limited knowledge about the relative appropriateness of different targeting models (for example, based on income status, geographic area, specific needs, or attributes) in different situations; poor data-collection and data-analysis capacities; a lack of reliable screening instruments; and poor public awareness and education. Reflecting broader concerns in the field, Aryeetey and Goldstein and Raczynski underscore the need for greater capacity-building, training, and needs assessments in this area.

A fourth issue concerns the mechanisms for identifying and engaging target groups. Recent critical reviews of targeting strategies have underscored that these are frequently oriented by demand-driven models with unrealistic assumptions about the initiative and start-up resources of targeted groups. Thus, for example, Aryeetey and Goldstein emphasize that initiatives undertaken through the Program of Action to Mitigate the Social Costs of Adjustment in Ghana failed principally because they were demand oriented, and the poorest groups were consequently unable to meet qualifying requirements. Similarly, Hunsley notes that the introduction of copayment requirements, or user fees, in Canada may dissuade some groups from seeking necessary assistance. Finally, a related observation can be made in connection with the shift from supply- to demand-driven subsidies, as detailed in Raczynski's discussion of reforms in the Chilean health and education sectors. In that instance, the failure to calibrate subsidies to real price and cost levels encouraged inflationary billing and accounting practices that resulted in unexpected efficiencies and distortions. Overall, these studies suggest that the social and economic objectives of targeting strategies must be articulated with the context, resources, and strategies that inform their implementation.

The nature and, more specifically, the complexity of the social-welfare system constitutes another challenge for targeting policies highlighted in the case studies of this book. The Canadian experience provides a case in point. In Canada, a country with an extensive and highly institutionalized social safety net, social-policy reforms currently entail a shift away from universalist principles to more stringent means testing and tighter eligibility requirements, particularly in the area of income support and social assistance. As Hunsley explains, however, such changes are producing reduced benefits and increased social hardship, a trend that is equally evident in the developing world. In addition, the very complexity of the system and programs means that tightening the benefits in some areas entails greater efforts to access benefits and greater dependency in others. As Hunsley (this volume, p. 105) summarizes,

> Program costs are ... being pushed from one source to another in a system that is becoming more complex. Because of the combinations of benefits and accessible services, removing candidates from one program may result in as many or more costs turning up elsewhere. For example, reductions in unemployment protection may trigger increases in social-assistance and disability-insurance costs. ... These risks increase when program benefits are narrowly targeted.

The result of targeting efforts in complex systems may be not so much the saving or targeting of resources as the unintended and unstrategic reallocation of them. This insight is interesting in light of Raczynski's observation that preexisting universal programs may facilitate subsequent moves to a targeted approach. Although this may be so in some cases, the Canadian experience suggests that the transition may nevertheless be anything but straightforward and may present obstacles of particular relevance to other postwelfare states. Again, as Hunsley notes, this issue presents important challenges for monitoring and assessment.

Finally, political factors are among the most persistent obstacles to effective targeting strategies. Most of the literature on targeting in both the North and the South has emphasized that people generally do not like to have their privileges withdrawn through redistributive efforts, such as through the withdrawal of food subsidies or the introduction of fees for health or education. In the Canadian case, the movement away from comprehensive, or universalist, social programs and principles has tended to provoke negative reactions from constituencies reluctant to lose access to, or to have to pay for, benefits or services long considered an entitlement. Opposition has come particularly from the left, which contends that reform trends — especially, concerted efforts to target some benefits more narrowly — fail to address more fundamental economic problems and represent a conservative willingness to stigmatize and shift blame to the poorest groups (Brodie 1994; Geller and Joel 1997; Pulkingham and Ternowetsky 1997, 1998). In the South, where the polarization of income-based poverty tends to be more pronounced and where universal social programs are less common or relevant, political obstacles to targeting are nevertheless also significant (UNRISD 1995). As we have seen in the cases of Chile and Ghana, efforts to redistribute resources within the health and education sectors have met with limited success, and the wealthiest strata have continued to benefit disproportionately from social expenditures.

Although the appropriate role of the state (versus the market or civil society) remains central to the current development debate and social-sector spending trends and levels continue to draw critical attention in the North and South, states everywhere retain an essential and inevitable responsibility for strategic resource allocation. As highlighted by the general record and the case studies in this volume, a number of conditions are likely to affect the success of efforts to achieve effective targeting and, especially, improved and more equitable social outcomes. These will include comparative examination and policy attention to various models for financing, designing, and implementating targeted programs; the technical needs and capacities that influence the practical articulation of these reforms; indicators and monitoring tools to comprehensively assess the social and economic benefits and costs of targeting measures; and the political factors that may facilitate or constrain the introduction and success of such strategies.

Democratization of social policy

A final, recurrent theme in the literature and in this volume concerns the democratization of social policy, or the articulation of participatory, responsive, and accountable approaches to social policy. Emphasis on the democratic nature of reforms derives from a number of factors. Particularly in the South, authoritarian governments have recently given way to new democracies with varying degrees of maturity and consolidation. Although support for democratic principles and practices is not as central to the neoliberal agenda as privatization, decentralization, or targeting efforts, it is nevertheless increasingly considered complementary to current reforms. Neoliberals concerned with ensuring stable economic climates, successful adjustment, and limited state intervention seem also to view measures to enhance popular participation and strengthen civil society as pragmatic and consistent with the dominant philosophy (Marcussen 1996; Ndegwa 1996; Allen 1997). Not surprisingly, moreover, the democratic character and implications of social and economic policy (and reform) draw equal attention and support from the other end of the ideological spectrum. As we have seen, critics of neoliberal adjustment perceive increased governmental accountability and popular involvement in policy as prerequisites for more sustainable development strategies, particularly in the wake of adjustment experiments the critics perceive as externally imposed and socially costly.

If some degree of consensus exists about the value of democratically oriented reform, albeit differently premised in each case, the experience of adjustment in both the North and the South nevertheless underscores some important issues for consideration. Again, for those concerned with elaborating more socially and economically feasible models of development, attention to contradictions between the stated objectives of policy and the conditions for, and experience of, implementation appear critical. One area in which contradictions are of increasing concern is that of the decentralization of social policy, a theme addressed above. Both in the development literature and in Northern discourse, the concepts of decentralization and democratization have either explicitly or implicitly been invoked interchangeably and presumed to represent mutually reinforcing trends. As our case studies show, in Ghana, Chile, and to some extent Canada, the deconcentration of authority and responsibility for social policy from central to local levels has often been thought to be justified because it presents an opportunity to promote civic engagement, enhance program efficiency, and strengthen government responsiveness.

Despite such arguments, however, empirical analyses of decentralization show that its political implications are less clear. Current studies challenge the predominant assumption that decentralization strengthens democracy by more directly engaging nongovernmental actors in the processes of policy-making. These studies are instead deconstructing, or "unpacking," the concept of civil society, using analyses that underscore the fact that relations of power and privilege, rather than wholly egalitarian principles and practices, characterize and differentiate civil society. For example, particularly in the South, those who observe that nongovernmental actors may in fact be elite oriented, urban based, male dominated, exclusionary, and vulnerable to corruption question the assumption that the decentralization of social policy will ensure equitable input and outcomes (UNRISD 1995; Stewart 1997).

As Aryeetey and Goldstein suggest in this volume, the new institutional arrangements for social policy in Ghana have presupposed the existence of local, representative political structures, rather than establishing them. Such local structures, particularly in the case of NGOs, often do not exist. Razcynski and other Latin American scholars have similarly pointed to the limits of decentralization, highlighting competing and persistent tendencies to centralize power and authority, clientelism, and co-optation (Oxhorn 1995; Veltmeyer 1997). Even in Canada, where democratic political institutions are well consolidated, the compatibility of decentralization with greater participation and responsiveness is not self-evident. Instead, as Hunsley argues, the rapidly expanding role of municipal and provincial governments, not to mention the "third sector," raises unresolved questions about the implications of these trends for patterns of interest representation and political accountability. Such observations are reinforced by a substantial body of work that emphasizes the weak record and capacities of local entities, particularly NGOs, to undertake reliable and comprehensive evaluations of their own work and ensure basic degrees of transparency (Smillie 1997). As these and other studies emphasize, reforms such as decentralization are causing shifts in the institutional frameworks for state–society interactions on policy matters. A range of contextual factors determine whether the consequences of such shifts are particularly democratic, and these contextual factors constitute an important area for study.

A second set of democratization issues concerns the values or ethical determinants of approaches to social-policy reform and the degree to which these are compatible with democracy and equality. Along with the need to strengthen institutional mechanisms for political participation, an equally fundamental priority for those concerned with the democratic content of reforms is to ensure that they are empowering and redistributive and serve to redress trends to socioeconomic exclusion. As Raczynski emphasizes in the case of Chile, government aspirations to sociopolitical integration imply policies to enhance the capabilities and resources of the poor and to ensure a basic level of welfare and citizenship for the population.

If notions of empowerment and redistribution are increasingly included as performance yardsticks for policy change and outcomes, the empirical record on reform to date again highlights some important questions for analysis. Most obviously — as we have seen in the cases of Ghana, Chile, and Canada — economic- and social-policy reforms to date have often served to exclude and disenfranchise vulnerable segments of society, rather than empowering them. In all three cases, poverty levels remained high and income polarization grew. Beyond such measurable or quantifiable indicators, however, some more abstract, but important, discursive trends have emerged that warrant consideration. As one analyst (Brodie 1994, p. 57) observed, the discourse of current reform trends

> is increasingly framed in terms of a new definition of citizenship which denies that the citizen can claim universal social rights from the state. The new common good is one which promotes efficiency and competition. In turn the good citizen is one who recognizes the limits and liabilities of state intervention and instead works longer and harder in order to become self-reliant. According to this vision, those who make group claims for compensatory justice ... are isolated as special interest groups who demand privileges that are unearned and which violate the new norms of citizenship.

Clearly, these reflections resonate most in the developed world: developing countries have historically been unable to provide universal social rights for their citizens. Still, as suggested implicitly throughout this volume, dominant reform philosophies in both the North and the South have not only accorded primacy to the market but also encouraged an erosion of the types of political and social claims that citizens can legitimately make on their states. By reducing public social spending and "offloading" greater responsibilities, particularly to nongovernmental groups and communities, societies in the developed and developing worlds are witnessing a greater privatization and individualization of risk and responsibility for social welfare.

For development-policy researchers in particular, these trends imply a need to illuminate and critically explore the values and assumptions underpinning developmental strategies and policy reforms in contrast to their stated aspirations to democratic and egalitarian social outcomes.

A broader, related type of research would build knowledge concerning competing views of social development and, by extension, various perceptions across countries and regions of the obligations of states and societies in the social realm. As Bhalla and Lapeyre (1997, p. 430) emphasized, "such notions as exclusion, well being, and welfare are society specific, and cannot be considered independently of the social and cultural norms and institutional context within which they are to be studied." MacPherson (cited in Patel 1992) made a similar point, suggesting that social policies are fundamentally the mechanisms used to redistribute resources and promote social development. To be effective, however, he says they must be founded on a set of guiding principles, which would ideally emerge from a wider debate within a society on its goals and vision of development. A study of these cross-national and cross-regional differences in public attitudes would contribute to defining policy contexts and priorities and, ultimately, to the sustainability of various policy options.

A final set of observations related to democracy and social-policy reform is more historical. These concern the types of state, particularly in the developing world, that have succeeded in achieving impressive levels of social development. Relevant in this context are current prescriptions for more "developmental" states, a term recently coined by Leftwich. The concept refers to those states that have "concentrated sufficient power, autonomy and capacity at the centre to shape, pursue and encourage the achievement of explicit developmental objectives" (Leftwich 1995, p. 401). This notion appears to be interchangeable with, and implicit in, recent calls at national and international levels for more "managerial" and "activist" governments that would be able and willing to pursue social development and economic growth concurrently.

Although recommendations that states be more developmental foster easy consensus in current development discourse, in general the development literature has given scant attention to identifying the relevant historical and political factors underlying such developmentalism. One troubling paradox, for example, is that significant strides in social development (for example, in China, Cuba, and Viet Nam) have been achieved by governments willing and able to bypass popular consent. A similar observation tends to be true of the NICs, which are regularly touted as models or hopeful alternatives for countries struggling with persistent poverty, inequality, and economic crisis. As Leftwich (1994) emphasized, the developmental states and, in particular, the

NICs have tended to have a common regime type or troublesome political-institutional features. Much of the current development literature fails to address this issue. Leftwich (1994, p. 368) explained that

> Uncomfortable as it may be to acknowledge, the model of the developmental state ... entails a strong and determined state which protects a powerful and competent bureaucracy that largely shapes and directs development policy, a dubious (and sometimes appalling) civil and human rights record, the suppression or control of civil society and a fusion — at least at the top — of the political direction of economic power. Above all, both the idea and practice of developmental states illustrate not simply the importance, but the primacy of politics and the state in development.

Pointing to one-party rule, insulated bureaucracies, and weak or controlled civil societies, Leftwich suggested that the states that have most successfully appeared to combine economic growth and social-development objectives have often tended to be less than democratic. Zuvekas (1997) complemented this analysis with other, cautionary observations, including the observation that the NICs began their own reform processes at much less pronounced levels of inequality than other developing areas, such as Latin America or Africa.

This is not meant to imply that democracy and higher levels of social development are intrinsically incompatible: the experience of OECD countries shows the contrary, as do the experiences of such countries as Chile, where some have observed that norms of political accountability have in fact prompted the newly democratic regime to court popular support to some degree through basic-needs strategies (Oxhorn 1995; IDRC–CIDA–UNRISD 1996). The suggestion here is more modest, that apolitical and ahistorical analyses should be avoided in future research, particularly comparative research, in the service of sustainable and balanced social and economic reform and that this research should pay attention to the real political-institutional factors that influence policy options, agendas, and development paths.

Conclusion

Deepening globalization and simultaneous adjustment of economies in the North and South have turned greater attention to the international and comparative dimensions of social policy. Reduced trade barriers, international capital flows and competitiveness, demographic trends, and revolutions in information and technology are just some of the forces reshaping the state's role in its domestic affairs.

For social policy, the implications are far reaching. Global trends are diminishing traditional notions of sovereignty. But more so they are encouraging a convergence of public-policy problems and options for countries in the developed and developing worlds. This is a central conclusion of this volume. Although Ghana, Chile, and Canada are countries in different regions and at quite different levels of economic and social development, the overviews in this volume of their recent experiences with neoliberal social-policy reforms highlight a range of common philosophies, policy trends, and challenges. These provide a potentially rich basis for shared perspectives, information exchange, and collaborative learning. In the broadest sense, the studies illustrate how governments in the North and South are linked in their pursuit of more sustainable, if as yet undetermined, ways to engage the state, the market, and civil society in ensuring the welfare of their societies.

In addition to highlighting the international relevance of these trends and offering a selective discussion of some outstanding issues and challenges for research on the recent economic and social-policy reforms, I have tried in this chapter to suggest something about the focus and character of future research agendas in this field. Specifically, I have argued that future research would benefit from the contribution of context-specific but comparative perspectives. Reflecting on the character of contemporary social-policy analysis generally, one author (Hill 1997, p. 8) expressed the problem as follows:

> The study of social policy [to date] ... has been concerned to examine the extent to which [states] meet people's needs. Often, indeed, studies of social policy go further, and explicitly analyze the extent to which they contribute to social equality. In this sense, an academic discipline has been built up with an explicitly political stance ... . [This] strong normative bias in the study of social policy has led at times to a greater pre-occupation with criticism of policies than with attempts to discover why they take the forms they do. In practice, if one believes that policies are wrong or ineffective, it is important to understand why this is so, particularly if one's objective is to change them.

These observations are salient to future approaches to social development and social-policy reform. Today, at international and national levels, theorists and practitioners are trying to articulate a new approach to development that particularly redresses the social costs of recent neoliberal reforms and embodies a more balanced and integrated approach to development. Progress is likely to require researchers to move beyond the polarized debates about structural adjustment that have for so long dominated the development literature. An important conclusion to be drawn from this volume is that the constructive assessment of social-policy reform and, by extension, the introduction of more feasible policy alternatives are likely to require due attention to contextual factors that shape policy choices, implementation processes, and social and economic outcomes.

Appendix 1

Acronyms and Abbreviations

AFPs	Administradoras de Fondos de Pensiones (administrators of pension funds) [Chile]
ASPR	Assessment of Social Policy Reform
CWIQ	Core Welfare Indicators Questionnaire [Ghana]
DPCU	District Planning Coordinating Unit [Ghana]
ENOWID	Enhancing Opportunities for Women in Development [Ghana]
ERP	Economic Recovery Program [Ghana]
FNDR	Fondo Nacional de Desarrollo Regionala (national regional development fund) [Chile]
FOSIS	Fondo de Solidaridad e Inversión Social (social solidarity and investment fund) [Chile]
GBP	pound sterling [United Kingdom]
GDP	gross domestic product
GLSS 1	first Ghana Living Standards Survey
GNP	gross national product
GSS	Ghana Statistical Service

HDI	Human Development Index [UNDP]
IFI	international financial institution
ISAPRE	Institucion de Salud Previsional (institution for provisional health) [Chile]
NAPPR	National Action Plan for Poverty Reduction [Ghana]
NDPC	National Development Planning Commission [Ghana]
NGO	nongovernmental organization
NIC	newly industrialized country
ODA	overseas development assistance
OECD	Organisation for Economic Co-operation and Development
OFY	Operation Feed Yourself [Ghana]
PAMSCAD	Program of Action to Mitigate the Social Costs of Adjustment [Ghana]
PPA	participatory poverty assessment
SIF	Social Investment Fund [Latin America]
SNS	Servicio Nacional de Salud (national health service) [Chile]
SOE	state-owned enterprise
UNDP	United Nations Development Programme
UNICEF	United Nations Children's Fund
UNRISD	United Nations Research Institute for Social Development
URADEP	Upper Region Agricultural Development Program [Ghana]
USD	United State dollar
USE	Unidad de Subsidio Escolar (unit for school subsidy) [Chile]

Appendix 2

Contributing Authors

Ernest Aryeetey
Associate Professor
Institute of Statistical, Social and
 Economic Research
University of Ghana
Legon, Ghana

Markus Goldstein
Research Associate
Institute of Statistical, Social and
 Economic Research
University of Ghana
Legon, Ghana

Graduate student
Department of Agricultural and
 Resource Economics
University of California
Berkeley, CA, USA

Terrance Hunsley
Research and Consulting Services
70 First Avenue
Ottawa, ON, Canada
K1S 2G2

Jennifer L. Moher
Research Associate
Assessment of Social Policy Reform
International Development Research
 Centre
Ottawa, ON, Canada

Daniel A. Morales-Gómez
Senior Scientist and Team Leader
Assessment of Social Policy Reform
International Development Research
 Centre
Ottawa, ON, Canada

Dagmar Raczynski
Sociologist and Senior Researcher
Corporación de Investigaciones
 Económicas para Latinoamérica
Casilla 16496, Correo 9
Santiago, Chile

Necla Tschirgi
Team Leader
Peace Building and Reconstruction
International Development Research
 Centre
Ottawa, ON, Canada

Bibliography

Afshar, H; Dennis, C., ed. 1992. Women and adjustment policies in the Third World. St. Martin's Press, New York, NY, USA.
Allen, C. 1997. Who needs civil society? Review of African Political Economy, 24(73), 329–337.
Amsden, A. 1989. Asia's next giant: South Korea and late industrialization. Oxford University Press, New York, NY, USA.
Arellano, J.P. 1985. Políticas sociales y desarrollo. Chile 1924–84. Ediciones Corporación de Investigaciones Económicas para Latinoamérica, Santiago, Chile.
Aryeetey, E. 1985. Decentralizing regional planning in Ghana. Dortmunder Beitraege zur Raumplanung, 42, Institut fuer Raumplanung, Universitaet Dortmund, Dortmund, Germany.
——— 1995. Aid effectiveness in Ghana. Report of a study sponsored by the Overseas Development Council, Washington, DC, USA. Overseas Development Council, Washington, DC, USA.

Bakker, I. 1994. The strategic silence: gender and economic policy. Zed Books, London, UK.
Bengoa, J. 1995. Chile. Equidad y excxusión, temas sociales. Sur Centro de Estudios Sociales y Educación, Santiago, Chile.
Berry, A. 1997. The income distribution threat in Latin America. Latin American Research Review, 32(2), 3–169.
Bhalla, A.; Lapeyre, F. 1997. Social exclusion: towards an analytical and operational framework. Development and Change, 28(3), 413–431.
Bitar, S. 1979. Transición, socialismo y democracia. La experiencia Chilena. Siglo XXIU Editores, Santiago, Chile.
Botchwey, K. 1995. Speech presented at the Plenary Conference of the Global Coalition for Africa — Africa's Future and the World — 27–28 Nov 1995, Maastricht, Netherlands. Global Coalition for Africa, Washington, DC, USA.
Brodie, J. 1994. Shifting the boundaries: gender and the politics of restructuring. In Bakker, I., ed., The strategic silence: gender and economic policy. Zed Books, London, UK. pp. 47–60.

Cabezas, M. 1988. Revisión metodológica y estadística del gasto social en Chile: 1970-86. Corporación de Investigaciones Económicas para Latinoamérica, Santiago, Chile. Notas Técnicas CIEPLAN, No. 114, May.

Castañeda, T. 1992. Combating poverty. Innovative social reforms in Chile during the 1980s. International Center for Economic Growth; ICS Press, San Francisco, CA, USA.

Celedón, C.; Oyarzo, C. 1998. Los desafíos en la salud. *In* Cortázar, R.; Vial, J., ed., Construyendo opciones. Propuestas económicas y sociales para el cambio de siglo. Corporación de Investigaciones Económicas para Latinoamérica-Ediciones Dolmen, Santiago, Chile.

Cheema, G.S.; Rondinelli, A.D., ed. 1983. Decentralization and development: policy implementation in developing countries. Sage Publications, Beverly Hills, CA, USA; London, UK.

CIDA-UNRISD-IDRC (Canadian International Development Agency; United Nations Research Institute for Social Development; International Development Research Centre). 1996. Social development in the developing world: the challenge of policy performance. Report of the CIDA-UNRISD-IDRC seminar, Social Development and Public Policies. IDRC, Ottawa, ON, Canada. 78 pp.

CIEPLAN-CORSAPS-FLACSO (Corporación de Investigaciones Económicas para Latinoamérica; Corporación de Salud y Politicas Sociales; Facultad Latinoamericana de Ciencias Sociales-Sede). 1996. Fundamentos para una reforma del sistema de seguridad social en salud. Diagnóstico y recomendaciones. Proyecto Ministerio de Salud sobre Evaluación de la Factibilidad Económica y Política de la Reforma de la Seguridad Social en Salud. Santiago, Chile. Informe de Avance, No. 1.

Clark, J. 1992. Democratizing development: the role of voluntary organizations. Kumarian Press, West Hartford, CT, USA.

CNSP (Consejo Nacional para la Superación de la Pobreza). 1996. La pobreza en Chile. Un desafío de equidad e integración social, informe, consejo nacional para la superación de la pobreza. Agosto, Santiago, Chile.

Conyers, D. 1983. Decentralization: the latest fashion in development administration? Public Administration and Development, 3, 97-109.

Cook, P.; Kirkpatrick, C. 1997. Introduction and overview: privatization and public enterprise reform in developing countries — the World Bank's *Bureaucrats in Business Report.* Journal of International Development, 9(6), 843-895.

Cortázar, R. 1977. Necesidades básicas y extrema pobreza. Programa de Empleo para Latinoamérica y el Caribe, Santiago, Chile. Investigaciones sobre Empleo No. 5.

―――― 1994. Política laboral en el Chile democrático. Avances y Desafíos en los Noventa. Ediciones Dolmen, Santiago, Chile.

Cox, C. 1997. La reforma de la educación Chilena: contextos, contenidos, implementación. Corporación de Investigaciones Económicas para Latinoamérica, Santiago, Chile. Colección Estudios CIEPLAN, No. 45, Jun.

Crispi, J.; Marcel, M. 1993. Aspectos cuantitativos de la política social en Chile 1987–1993. Dirección de Presupuesto, Ministerio de Hacienda, Santiago, Chile. Documento de Trabajo.
CSO (Central Statistics Office). 1991. Quarterly digest of statistics (June). CSO, Harare, Zimbabwe.
——— 1994. Quarterly digest of statistics (March). CSO, Harare, Zimbabwe.

De Kadt, E. 1993. Poverty focused policies. The experience of Chile. Institute of Development Studies, University of Sussex, Brighton, Sussex, UK. Discussion Paper No. 319, Jan.
Demery, L.; Chao, S.; Bernier, R.; Mehra, K. 1995. The incidence of social spending in Ghana. World Bank, Washington, DC, USA. Poverty and Social Policy Discussion Paper No. 82.
Dowbor, L. 1998. Decentralization and governance. Latin American Perspectives, 25(1), 28–43.

ECLAC (Economic Commission for Latin America and the Caribbean). 1995. Modelos de desarrollo, papel del estado y políticas sociales: nuevas tendencias en América Latina. División de Desarrollo Social, Santiago, Chile. LC/R.1575, 7 Sep.
Esping-Anderson, G. 1990. The three worlds of welfare capitalism. Cambridge; Polity Press, London, UK.
Espínola, V. 1991. Descentralización del sistema escolar en Chile. Centro de Investigaciones y Desarrollo de la Educación, Santiago, Chile.

Foxley, A. 1983. Latin American experiments in neoconservative economics. University of California Press, Berkeley, CA, USA.
Foxley, A.; Aninat, E.; Arellano, J.P. 1979. Redistributive effects of government programs. Pergamon Press, Oxford, UK.

Garretón, M.A. 1994. New state–society relations in Latin America. In Bradford, ed., Redefining the state in Latin America. Organisation for Economic Co-operation and Development, Paris, France.
Geller, G.; Joel, J. 1997. Struggling for citizenship in the global economy: bond raters versus women and children. In Pulkingham, J.; Ternowetsky, G., ed., Remaking Canadian social policy: social security in the late 1990s. Fernwood Publishing, Halifax, NS, Canada. pp. 303–315.
Glewwe, P.; Jacoby, H. 1992. Estimating the determinants of cognitive achievement in low-income countries: the case of Ghana. World Bank, Washington, DC, USA. Living Standards Measurement Study, Working Paper No. 91.
Glover, D. 1991. A layman's guide to structural adjustment. Canadian Review of Development Studies, 12(1), 173–185.
GOG (Government of Ghana). 1964. Seven year development plan 1963/64–1969/70. GOG, Accra, Ghana.

Green, D. 1996. Latin America: neoliberal failure and the search for alternatives. Third World Quarterly, 17(1), 109–121.

Grosh, M. 1992. From platitude to practice: targeting social programs in Latin America. Human Research Division, Latin American and Caribbean Technical Department, Regional Studies Program, World Bank, Washinton DC, USA. Report No. 21, Sep.

GSS (Ghana Statistical Service). 1995. The pattern of poverty in Ghana. Ghana Extended Poverty Study, Accra, Ghana.

Haindl, E.; et al. 1989. Gasto social efectivo. Un instrumento que asegura la superación definitiva de la pobreza crítica. Universidad de Chile, Facultad de Ciencias Económicas y Administrativas y Oficina de Planificación Nacional, Presidencia de la República, Santiago, Chile.

Hill, M. 1997. Understanding social policy (5th ed.). Blackwell Publishers, Cambridge, UK.

Howes, M.; Sattar, M. 1992. Bigger and better? Scaling up strategies pursued by BRAC 1972–1991. In Howes, M.; Sattar, M., ed., Making a difference: NGOs and development in a changing world. Earthscan, London, UK.

Hunsley, T. 1997a. Incomes and outcomes, lone parents and social policy in ten countries. McGill–Queen's Press, Kingston, ON, Canada.

———— 1997b. Disability programs: considerations on cost and coordination. Institute for Work and Health, Toronto, ON, Canada. Occasional Paper.

———— ed. 1992. Social policy and the global economy. Queen's University School of Policy Studies, Kingston, ON, Canada.

Illy, H.F. 1985. Decentralization as a tool for development? Notes on the current debate. The Speyer School of Administrative Sciences, Speyer, Germany. Mimeo.

ISSER (Institute of Statistical Social and Economic Research). 1994. State of the Ghanaian economy report 1993. University of Ghana, Legon, Ghana.

———— 1996. State of the Ghanaian economy report 1995. University of Ghana, Legon, Ghana.

Johnson, J.; Wasty, S.S. 1993. Borrower ownership of adjustment programs and the political economy of reform. World Bank, Washington DC, USA. World Bank Discussion Paper No. 199.

Jolly, R.; et al. 1992. Adjustment revisited. World Development, 19(2).

Karger, H. 1996. The public good and the welfare state in Africa. Journal of Social Development in Africa, 11(1), 5–14.

Kelly, T. 1997. Public expenditures and growth. Journal of Development Studies, 34(1), 60–80.

Kliksberg, B., ed. 1994. El rediseño del estado. Una perspectiva internacional. Instituto Nacional de Administración Pública de México–Fondo de Cultura Económica, Mexico City, Mexico.

Kwadzo, G.T.M.; Kumekpor, M.L. 1994. PAMSCAD evaluation (CIDA supported programs). Canadian International Development Agency, Ottawa, ON, Canada.

Kwapong, A.A.; et al. 1996. An assessment of national capacity-building in Ghana. Report of a study prepared by the National Capacity-Building Assessment Group for the World Bank, Accra, Ghana. World Bank, Washington, DC, USA.

Larrañaga, O. 1994. Pobreza. Crecimiento y desigualdad: Chile 1987–92. Revista de Análisis Económico, 9(2).

Leftwich, A. 1994. Governance, the state, and the politics of development. Development and Change, 25, 363–386.

——— 1995. Bringing politics back in: towards a model of the developmental state. Journal of Development Studies, 31(3).

MacKintosh, M. 1995. Competition and contracting in selective social provisioning. European Journal of Development Research, 7(1), 26–50.

Marcel, M. 1997. Políticas públicas en democracia: el caso de la reforma tributaria de 1990 en Chile. Corporación de Investigaciones Económicas para Latinoamérica, Santiago, Chile. Colección Estudios CIEPLAN, No. 45, Jun.

Marcel, M.; Arenas, A. 1991. Reformas a la seguridad social en Chile. Inter-American Development Bank, Washington DC, USA. Serie de Monografías, No. 5.

Marcussen, H.S. 1996. NGOs, the state and civil society. Review of African Political Economy, 69, 405–423.

Marshall, J. 1981. Gasto público en Chile, 1969–79. Metodología y resultados. Corporación de Investigaciones Económicas para Latinoamérica, Santiago, Chile. Notas Técnicas CIEPLAN, No. 33, Jul.

Maxwell, J. 1996. Social dimensions of economic growth – part 1. CABE News, 6–10.

McKay, A. 1997. Poverty reduction through economic growth: some issues. Journal of International Development, 9(4), 665–673.

Mesa-Lago, C. 1978. Social security in Latin America: pressure groups, stratification and inequality. University of Pittsburgh Press. Pittsburgh, PA, USA.

MHDP (Ministerio de Hacienda, Dirección de Presupuesto). 1997. Estadísticas de las finanzas públicas 1987–1996. MHDP, Santiago, Chile.

MIDEPLAN (Ministerio de Planificación y Cooperación). 1996. Balance de seis años de las políticas sociales 1990–1996. MIDEPLAN, Santiago, Chile.

——— n.d. Encuesta CASEN. MIDEPLAN, Santiago, Chile. Various years.

Mikell, G. 1991. Equity issues in Ghana's rural development. *In* Rothchild, D., ed., The political economy of recovery. SAIS African Studies Library; Lynne Rienner Publishers, Boulder, CO, USA; London, UK.

Miranda, E. 1990. Descentralización y privatización del sistema de salud Chileno. Centro de Estudios Públicos, Santiago, Chile. Estudios Públicos No. 39, winter.

Mishra, R. 1984. The welfare state in crisis: social thought and social change. Wheatsheaf Books, London, UK.

Monckeberg, F. 1984. Evolución de la desnutrición y mortalidad infantil en Chile en los últimos años. Revista Creces, 10.

Muñoz, O.; et al. 1980. Crecimiento y estructura del empleo público en Chile: 1940–1970. Corporación de Investigaciones Económicas para Latinoamérica, Santiago, Chile. Notas Técnicas CIEPLAN, No. 22, Jan.

Ndegwa, S.N. 1996. The two faces of civil society: NGOs and the politics in Africa. Kumerian Press, West Hartford, CT, USA.

Norton, A.; et al. 1995. Poverty assessment in Ghana using qualitative and participatory research methods. World Bank, Washington, DC, USA. PSP Discussion Paper Series, No. 83.

Nyong, M. 1994. Government interventionism, privatization, and economic development: a critical review of the issues. African Review of Money, Finance and Banking, 1, 123–138.

ODEPLAN (Oficina de Planificatión Nacional); Universidad Católica de Chile. 1975. Mapa de la externa pobreza. Universidad Católica de Chile, Santiago, Chile.

OECD (Organisation for Economic Co-operation and Development). n.d. Main economic indicators. OECD, Paris, France. Various years.

Oxhorn, P. 1995. Organizing civil society: popular organizations and the struggle for democracy in Chile. The Pennsylvania State University Press, Pittsburgh, PA, USA.

PAL (Programa de Asistencia Legislativa). 1994. La productividad en la salud pública. PAL, Santiago, Chile. Bitácora Legislativa, No. 127, Aug.

Patel, L. 1992. Restructuring social welfare: options for South Africa. Ravan Press, Johannesburg, South Africa.

Pizarro, C.; Raczynski, D; Vial, J., ed. 1995. Políticas económicas y sociales en el Chile democrático. Corporación de Investigaciones Económicas para Latinoamérica–United Nations Children's Fund, Santiago, Chile.

Post, U.; Preuss, H. 1997. No miracle weapon for development. Development and Cooperation, 6, 4–5.

Power, G. 1997. Globalization and its discontents. Development, 40(2), 75–79.

Pulkingham, J.; Ternowetsky, G. 1997. The changing landscape of social policy and the Canadian welfare state. *In* Pulkingham, J.; Ternowetsky, G., ed.,

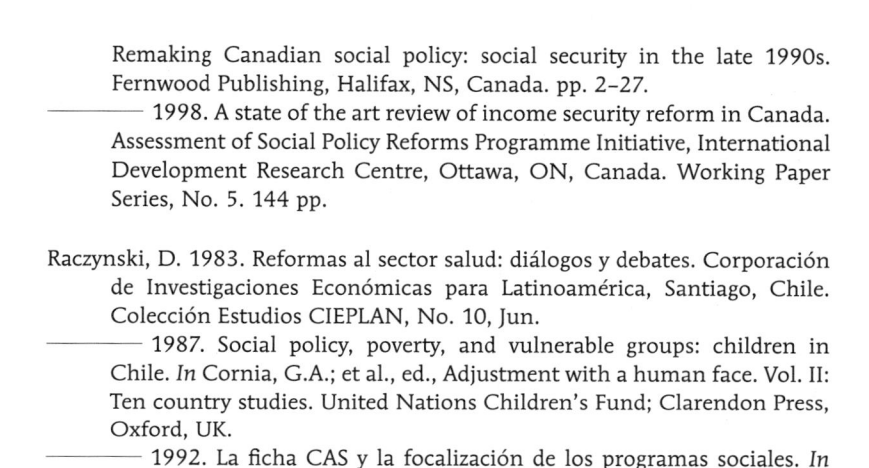

Remaking Canadian social policy: social security in the late 1990s. Fernwood Publishing, Halifax, NS, Canada. pp. 2–27.

———— 1998. A state of the art review of income security reform in Canada. Assessment of Social Policy Reforms Programme Initiative, International Development Research Centre, Ottawa, ON, Canada. Working Paper Series, No. 5. 144 pp.

Raczynski, D. 1983. Reformas al sector salud: diálogos y debates. Corporación de Investigaciones Económicas para Latinoamérica, Santiago, Chile. Colección Estudios CIEPLAN, No. 10, Jun.

———— 1987. Social policy, poverty, and vulnerable groups: children in Chile. In Cornia, G.A.; et al., ed., Adjustment with a human face. Vol. II: Ten country studies. United Nations Children's Fund; Clarendon Press, Oxford, UK.

———— 1992. La ficha CAS y la focalización de los programas sociales. In Gómez, S., ed., La realidad en cifras. Ediciones FLACSO-INE-UNRISD, Santiago, Chile. Estadísticas Sociales.

———— 1994. Social policies in Chile: origin, transformation, and perspectives. Helen Kellogg Institute for International Studies, University of Notre Dame, Notre Dame, IN, USA. Democracy and Social Policy Series, Working Paper No. 4.

———— 1995a. Estrategia para combatir la pobreza en América Latina: programas, instituciones y recursos. Corporación de Investigaciones Económicas para Latinoamérica; Inter-American Development Bank, Santiago de Chile.

———— 1995b. Focalización de programas sociales. Lecciones de la experiencia Chilena. In Pizarro, C.; et al., ed., Políticas económicas y sociales en el Chile democrático. Corporación de Investigaciones Económicas para Latinoamérica–United Nations Children's Fund, Santiago, Chile. [English version in 1996, Social and economic policies in Chile's transition to democracy.]

———— 1997. Social policies in Chile: transformation and perspectives. Paper presented at the Conference on Social Policies for the Urban Poor in Latin America: Welfare Reform in a Democratic Context, Sep 1997. The Helen Kellogg Institute for International Studies, Notre Dame, IN, USA.

———— 1998a. The crisis of old models of social protection in Latin America and new alternatives for dealing with poverty. In O'Donnell, G.; Tokman V., ed., Poverty and inequality in Latin America: issues and new challenges. Helen Kellogg Institute for International Studies, University of Notre Dame, Notre Dame, IN, USA.

———— 1998b. Para combatir la pobreza en Chile. Esfuerzos del pasado y desafíos presentes. In Cortázar, R.; Vial, J., ed., Construyendo opciones. Propuestas económicas y sociales para el cambio de siglo. Corporación de Investigaciones Económicas para Latinoamérica–Ediciones Dolmen, Santiago, Chile.

Raczynski, D.; Cabezas, M. 1988. Ingresos y gastos municipales: Chile (1977–87) y Gran Santiago (1985–87). Corporación de Investigaciones Económicas para Latinoamérica, Santiago. Chile. Notas Técnicas CIEPLAN, No. 121, Oct.

Raczynski, D.; Oyarzo, C. 1981. Por qué cae la tasa de mortalidad infantil en Chile? Corporación de Investigaciones Económicas para Latinoamérica, Santiago, Chile. Colección Estudios CIEPLAN, No. 6, Dec.

Raczynski, D.; Romaguera, P. 1995. Chile: poverty, adjustment, and social policies in the 1980s. In Lustig, N., ed., Coping with austerity: poverty and inequality in Latin America. The Brookings Institution, Washington, DC, USA.

Raczynski, D.; Serrano, C. 1985. Vivir la pobreza: testimonio de mujeres. Corporación de Investigaciones Económicas para Latinoamérica, Santiago, Chile.

——— 1987. Administración y gestión local. La experiencia de algunos municipios en Santiago. Corporación de Investigaciones Económicas para Latinoamérica, Santiago, Chile. Colección Estudios CIEPLAN, No. 22, Dec.

——— 1988. ¿Planificación para el desarrollo local? La experiencia de algunos municipios en Santiago. Corporación de Investigaciones Económicas para Latinoamérica, Santiago, Chile. Colección Estudios CIEPLAN, No. 24, Jun.

Richards, D.G. 1997. The political economy of the Chilean miracle. Latin American Research Review, 32(1).

Riveros, L. 1984. Distribución del ingreso, empleo y políticas sociales en Chile. Centro de Estudios Públicos, Santiago, Chile. Documento de Trabajo, No. 25, Mar.

Schellenberg, G.; Ross, D.P. 1977. Left poor by the market: a look at family poverty and earnings. Canadian Council on Social Development, Ottawa, ON, Canada.

Schkolnik, M. 1992. The distributive impact of fiscal and labour market policies: Chile's 1990–1 reforms. Florence, Italy. Innocenti Occasional Papers. Economic Policy Series, No. 33, Nov.

Sen, G. 1996. Gender, markets and states: a selective review and research agenda. World Development, 24(5), 821–831.

Serrano, C. 1995. Municipio, política social y pobreza. In Pizarro, C.; et al., ed., Políticas económicas y sociales en el Chile democrático. Corporación de Investigaciones Económicas para Latinoamérica–United Nations Children's Fund, Santiago, Chile.

——— 1996. Gobierno regional e inversión pública descentralizada. Corporación de Investigaciones Económicas para Latinoamérica, Santiago, Chile. Collección Estudios CIEPLAN, No. 42, Jun.

Sherraden, M. 1995. Social policy in Latin America. Latin American Research Review, 30(1), 176–190.

Sinha, R. 1995. Economic reform in developing countries: some conceptual issues. World Development, 23(4), 557-575.
Smeeding, T. 1996. Trends in income inequality: new evidence from the Luxembourg income study. Paper presented at the International Institute on Social Policy, Queen's University at Kingston, Kingston, ON, Canada.
Smillie, I. 1997. NGOs and development assistance: a change in mindset? Third World Quarterly, 18(3), 563-579.
Sojo, A. 1990. Naturaleza y selectividad de la política social. Revista de la CEPAL, 41.
Spicker, P. 1995. Social policy: themes and approaches. Prentice Hall-Harvester Wheatsheaf, Hertfordshire, UK.
Stahl, K. 1996. Anti-poverty programs: making structural adjustment more palatable. Report on social policy. NACLA Report on the Americas, 29(6), 32-36.
StatsCan. 1997. Social trends. Supply and Services Canada, Ottawa, ON, Canada.
Stewart, S. 1997. Happy ever after in the marketplace: non-government organizations and uncivil society. Review of African Political Economy, 71, 11-31.
Stewart, F.; Ranis, G. 1992. Decentralization in Chile. Department of Economics, Yale University, New Haven, CT, USA.
Streeten, P. 1979. From growth to basic needs. *In* Basic needs strategy as a planning parameter. German Foundation for International Development, Berlin, Germany. Mimeo.
Subramaniam, V. 1980. Developing countries. *In* Rowat, D., ed., International handbook on local government reorganization. Greenwood Press, Westport, CT, USA. Chapt. 47.

Torche, A. 1987. Distribuir el ingreso para satisfacer las necesidades básicas. *In* Larraín, L., ed., Desarrollo económico para Chile en democracia. Ediciones Universidad Católica, Santiago, Chile.
Toye, J. 1991. Ghana. *In* Mosley, P.; Harrigan, J.; Toye, J., ed., Aid and power: the World Bank and policy-based lending, vol. 2. Routledge, London, UK.
Tsie, B. 1996. States and markets in the Southern African Development Community (SADC): beyond the neoliberal paradigm. Journal of Southern African Studies, 22(1), 75-98.

UNDP (United Nations Development Programme). 1993a. Development cooperation report for Ghana 1989, 1991, 1993. Oxford University Press, New York, NY, USA.
―――― 1993b. Human development report 1993. Oxford University Press, New York, NY, USA.
―――― 1997. Human development report 1997. Oxford University Press, New York, NY, USA. 245 pp.

UNICEF (United Nations Children's Fund). 1986. Adjustment policies and programmes to protect children and other vulnerable groups. UNICEF, Accra, Ghana.

United Nations. 1995. Report of the World Summit for Social Development, Copenhagen, Sweden. United Nations, New York, NY, USA. 133 pp.

UNRISD (United Nations Research Institute for Social Development). 1995. States of disarray: the social effects of globalization. UNRISD, Geneva, Switzerland. 172 pp.

Veltmeyer, H. 1997. Decentralization as the institutional basis for community based participatory development: the Latin American experience. Canadian Journal of Development Studies, 28(2), 303–321.

Vergara, P. 1990. Políticas hacia la extrema pobreza en Chile, 1973–88. Facultad Latinoamericana de Ciencias Sociales-Sede, Santiago, Chile.

Vilas, C. 1996. Neoliberal social policy: managing poverty somehow. NACLA Report on the Americas, 29(6), 16–25.

Wade, R. 1990. Governing the market: economic theory and the role of government in Taiwan's industrialization. Princeton University Press, Princeton, NJ, USA.

WCSD (World Conference on Social Development). 1995. World development report 1995. Oxford University Press, New York, NY, USA.

Weyland, K. 1997 "Growth with equity" in Chile's new democracy. Latin American Research Review, 32(1).

World Bank. 1995a. Ghana: poverty past, present and future. Population and Human Resource Division, West Central Africa Department, Washington, DC, USA. Report No. 14504-GH.

———— 1995b. World development report, 1995. Oxford University Press, New York, NY, USA.

Zuvekas, C. 1997. Latin America's struggle for equitable economic adjustment. Latin American Research Review, 32(2).

About the Institution

The International Development Research Centre (IDRC) is committed to building a sustainable and equitable world. IDRC funds developing-world researchers, thus enabling the people of the South to find their own solutions to their own problems. IDRC also maintains information networks and forges linkages that allow Canadians and their developing-world partners to benefit equally from a global sharing of knowledge. Through its actions, IDRC is helping others to help themselves.

About the Publisher

IDRC Books publishes research results and scholarly studies on global and regional issues related to sustainable and equitable development. As a specialist in development literature, IDRC Books contributes to the body of knowledge on these issues to further the cause of global understanding and equity. IDRC publications are sold through its head office in Ottawa, Canada, as well as by IDRC's agents and distributors around the world. The full catalogue is available at http://www.idrc.ca/books/index.html.